Praise for *through*

Stephen Crippen brings intimate biography to Scripture to create a remarkable portrayal of the need for genuine remorse and the life-giving possibilities such remorse creates. Each sentence is carefully chosen and elegantly constructed. The result is an encounter with the author and with God that can be life changing for the reader. Any Christian serious about authentic living should read this book.

> —The Very Rev. Ian S. Markham, PhD, professor of theology and ethics, dean, and president of Virginia Theological Seminary

In *Remorse: Finding Joy through Honest Apology*, Stephen Crippen reclaims remorse not as a toxic version of shame, but as a window toward a deeper and more complex spirituality. Crippen's own story of remorse and, ultimately, self-compassion allows the reader to examine their own regret and guilt, trusting that this work can lead toward deeper joy. This is an excellent resource for those who want to rebuild a life of joy even after their emotional and spiritual foundations have been shattered by shame.

> —Rev. Dr. Brooke Petersen, lecturer in pastoral theology and director of master's programs at the Lutheran School of Theology at Chicago; author of *Religious Trauma: Queer Stories in Estrangement and Return*

I have personally worked with the Rev. Stephen Crippen for the past fifteen years. He is a brilliant mind, and a deeply compassionate one as well. He is a teacher, preacher, and counselor. This book takes up a topic that is so vital for wellness in each soul and in organizations as well. I highly commend this good work. Whether a pastor, leader, counselor, or friend, you will benefit as a human being from the wisdom in this book.

—The Rt. Rev. Gregory H. Rickel VIII, former bishop of the Episcopal Diocese of Olympia, Seattle, Washington

Gently, persistently, lovingly, Stephen Crippen guides us to face our fear of our own guilt and discover remorse as a path not to shame but to joy. This is a beautiful book, one I'd recommend for anyone who has ever had anything to feel sorry about. Which is to say, for all of us.

—Rev. Dr. Stephen R. Shaver, rector of the Episcopal Church of the Incarnation, Santa Rosa, California; author of *Metaphors of Eucharistic Presence: Language, Cognition, and the Body of Christ*

"Remorse is a royal road to profound grace and fullness of joy for anyone who recognizes this simple truth: 'I did this thing, and I should not have done it.'" This exquisite sentence from the preface of Crippen's book was enough to make me want to plunge into my own experiences of remorse in the light of Crippen's approach. Learning about "feeling sorry," "thinking sorry," "saying sorry," and "doing sorry" was both helpful and authentic. And, as the author suggests, joy awaits us along this road.

—The Most Rev. Melissa Skelton, assisting bishop of the
Episcopal Diocese of Olympia, Seattle, Washington

In a time when many parish leaders, lay and ordained, avoid challenging issues for fear that discussion—honest discussion—will drive people away, there is welcome relief in reading Stephen Crippen's sustained reflection on remorse and joy. In a time when many in the churches want to hear nothing of personal failure and recovery, here we encounter not the scolding voice of the cleric, but the wisdom and love and honesty that evoke and gently provoke. Here we encounter the rare blend of candor and wit, and sustained theological reflection interwoven with biography. Oh, that there were *more* of this writing in the church today! Take up and read this book that speaks of nothing less than the resurrection of life.

—Rev. Dr. Samuel Torvend, OblSB, professor of religion,
Pacific Lutheran University, Tacoma, Washington

Remorse

Remorse

Finding
Joy
through
Honest
Apology

Stephen Crippen

Fortress Press

Minneapolis

REMORSE
Finding Joy through Honest Apology

Cover design and illustration: Brad Norr Design

Print ISBN: 978-1-5064-7910-1
eBook ISBN: 978-1-5064-7911-8

For Michael D., who was just doing his job one night.
You saved my life.

CONTENTS

CONTENTS

PREFACE

I have attended hundreds of Alcoholics Anonymous meetings over the past nine years, and I have documentation of my attendance at the first few hundred in the form of court-ordered "meeting slips." About halfway through each meeting, the secretary says something like, "It's time for our Seventh Tradition," and starts passing a basket around the room for monetary donations. (The Seventh Tradition is, "Every AA group ought to be fully self-supporting, declining outside contributions."[1]) If you were court-ordered to attend AA meetings, as I was for a year beginning in May 2013, you would place your blank attendance slip (I got mine from my outpatient rehab clinic) into the basket along with your few dollars. After the secretary collected the basket and counted the money, they signed the slips, put them in the basket, and sent them back around the room.

These Seventh Tradition baskets remind me of offering plates at churches and were early objects of reflection for me in my effort to make theological sense of my recovery from alcoholism. The church offering plates typically are fancier, sometimes even lined with red velvet. (One of them in my history of churchgoing—and to my own amusement—has 2 Corinthians 9:7b carved along its ornate wooden edge: "God loves a cheerful giver." Another church I served pours all the collected money into soft maroon velvet bags, lending a dignified elegance to their presentation at the altar.) Despite these stylistic differences, church offering plates are sent around their rooms at about the same time as the AA baskets, approximately halfway through the service/meeting. Both are used as part of an organization's effort to support itself through the financial commitments of its members. The contributions they collect for both groups are generally understood to be expressions of gratitude, not tuition or admission. They support not-for-profit organizations that serve a spiritual—if not necessarily religious—purpose.

Yet the people who pass offering plates are usually upstairs in church buildings, and those who drop a few bucks into an AA basket usually gather downstairs, or in a less attractive room down a hall. The upstairs people are generally more comfortable with (and in many cases enthusiastic about) theology and religion. On the other hand, many people in recovery find little or no use for theology, religion, or churches, and have experienced faith communities as either unhelpfully judgmental or (in happier stories) ridiculously irrelevant. The AA literature is deliberately nonsectarian; there is even a reassuring chapter titled "To Agnostics" in *Alcoholics Anonymous*, the primary text of AA, usually called "The Big Book." The organization takes great pains to welcome those who have no faith or have been harmed by people of faith. And yet AA was created with the help of an Episcopal priest, and the ethical framework of AA and other twelve-step groups would be broadly recognizable to the "upstairs people" who attend the churches, synagogues, and mosques that lend their meeting spaces to these gatherings.

This personal experience in AA alongside my church life began my years-long journey of reflection, reading, and writing about remorse. I was particularly intrigued that the AA program of recovery offers great spiritual benefits for those who are willing to confront and work with their own wrongdoing, and yet all the religious and sectarian sources for the spiritual program have been carefully scrubbed. Now, there are positive reasons for this: AA is expressly not only for Christians, let alone Christians of particular denominations. AA is for everyone who desires to stop drinking, and an explicit religious framework (Christian or not) would immediately frustrate that purpose. And AA began in the 1930s, when most Christian churches in the midwestern cities where AA first took hold may not have welcomed honest and open discussion of alcohol problems. Finally, even alcoholics like me who are deeply comfortable with organized religion can find it refreshing and surprisingly helpful to do personal spiritual work (like making a list of persons we have harmed and becoming willing to make amends to them) outside of the usual constructs of church, theology, and prayer. Sometimes it just feels cleaner, simpler, more honest, to do all that work by following a basic list of tasks that focuses exclusively on practical matters.

"But the upstairs people need this too," I often thought. For a few years in my early recovery, I attended AA meetings in the parish hall of the same congregation I served as a deacon. I would be upstairs on Sunday mornings and downstairs on Monday evenings. I once attended an AA meeting and saw my own handwriting on sheets of flipchart paper we had used the day before in a spiritual reflection exercise. I knew instinctively that the people I served on Sunday mornings and the people I joined on Monday evenings all needed to do what the Monday-evening people were doing. That particular church was fairly good at encouraging its members to confront their own wrongdoing, but I don't think I've served one congregation in my long history of lay and clergy ministry that comes close to the AA standard: in AA, everyone publicly acknowledges they are there because of their wrongdoing and because they hope to find peace and recovery by directly confronting it and making things right.

A THEOLOGY OF RECOVERY

By the time I marked my fourth sobriety anniversary—May 13, 2017—I was packing our house for our move to Virginia, where I planned to attend seminary in formation for the Episcopal priesthood. At that time I told myself, "I want to write a theology of recovery." I entered seminary with this ambition and soon found a systematic theology professor who eventually became my thesis advisor. At our first advising meeting, I brought books on the topic of recovery to her office. They were good books. The most prominent author was Gerald May, who wrote eloquently about spirituality and addiction. But my advisor told me that I would have to go deeper in my theological work on the topic. The books I brought to her office approached the topic pastorally—usually with great effectiveness—and were useful for people seeking comfort and good counsel about the many problems of addiction, but my task was different: I wanted to do systematic theology on the human experience of addiction and recovery. I wanted to explore the topic as a fundamental problem of faith, like the problem of innocent suffering, or the problems of sin and death. To bridge the upstairs and downstairs worlds of church and AA, I would need to find their common ground. As a therapist, I had given much thought over the years to substance abuse and recovery. But as I walked the road of my own recovery, my worlds began to converge. My personal experience of recovery became (and remains) a major source of theological insight and a lens for reading and understanding the Bible.

Of course, other pastors, theologians, and therapists have reflected on addiction and recovery from theological and biblical perspectives. I have heard many faith leaders say, "Everyone is addicted to *something*" in their hope that more and more people would do more of the work—and receive the spiritual benefits—that recovery from substance abuse offers. Addiction has even (I think accurately!) been framed as a form of idolatry, a theological category of human misbehavior for which Jewish teachers and faith leaders offer particularly insightful wisdom. In the wake of an Episcopal bishop's drunk-driving arrest (and subsequent conviction for manslaughter) in late 2014, many

Episcopalians began reflecting on the shared problem of addiction that can develop in large systems like congregations and even dioceses. Addiction is often rightly front and center as a major theological topic. Nevertheless, as I began writing what I originally had called "a theology of recovery," I slowly realized that my topic was broader. When I had sat in AA meetings thinking, "The upstairs people need this too!" I wasn't thinking about their need for recovery from addiction, even though that particular need was so central to my own experience. I was thinking about the universal human need to admit and work on our wrongdoing, of various kinds, of all kinds.

Many churches I know are not good at working on wrongdoing. We mumble our confessions most Sundays and hear that God has forgiven us, but we tend not to dwell on the topic. People in mainline churches can be bashful about their faith, particularly the texts and rituals that focus on wrongdoing, because it can seem not only uncool, but actively harmful. Perhaps we are afraid that others will see our church as judgmental, one of the "problem" churches, the very churches one hears a lot about in AA. As a priest responsible for choosing which confession in the *Book of Common Prayer* we will use in worship, I once received a complaint that the particular confession I had chosen was deeply upsetting because it implied (in this person's view) that the gathered faithful should be ashamed of themselves. The phrase they took issue with was, "The evil we have done, and the evil done on our behalf."[2] The person said they "wanted to run screaming from the room" when the time came for us to recite this confession.

For both theological and pastoral reasons, I sympathize with this worshipper's reaction. In many of my sermons and other writings, I insist that I do not want to shame anyone, and I will reflect on shame in this book as well, holding it in sharp contrast to healthy and grace-filled remorse. And yet, when the day came for me to start writing my thesis and I decided to simply start writing something—anything—to get the first words on the blank page of my laptop, I wrote this paragraph, which survived nearly intact in the final thesis:

We should be ashamed of ourselves. Someone is to blame, and that person should take responsibility for their own wrongdoing. Ambivalent—or worse, nonexistent—remorse mocks the victim and fraudulently exonerates the offender, damaging the humanity of both. Hasty, facile appeals to grace and forgiveness, or even the well-intentioned empathetic sentiment "Well, we have all sinned and fallen short of the glory of God" may inflict further trauma upon everyone involved, while revealing the ulterior motive of those who rush to pardon: a desire to deny the brutal truth of what happened and avoid the terrible questions about humanity and God that haunt those who confront the truth. If the victim is dead, particularly if that death was caused by the offense, hasty pastoral reassurance of God's love and compassion for the killer could inflict further harm on the victim's survivors, driving them yet further from the everlasting arms of God. But terrible acts need not generate a body count to be terrible: a wicked word devastates; a mean-spirited rejection traumatizes; a selfish theft, even a petty one, destroys trust and deprives the victim of serenity. We should be ashamed of ourselves. Remorse matters.

The parishioner who complained about my choice of a confession text would likely (and perhaps justifiably) critique me for trying to have it both ways: I don't want to make people feel shame, and I take pains to differentiate chronic shame from healthy remorse, rejecting the former as harmful. And yet I began my first lengthy theological exploration of remorse with the sentence, "We should be ashamed of ourselves"! And I left it in! But I did attempt to explain myself in a footnote, and perhaps that footnote would encourage my parishioner (and you who are reading this now) to stay with me. Here's the footnote:

This paragraph was difficult, if oddly gratifying, to write. It pushes harshly against internal urges to reassure congregants in the pews, to announce "Good News," to simply be liked. This [thesis] is, in its essence, an attempt to notice those urges, acknowledge their usefulness, and gently but firmly move them to one side, so that a more profound— if excruciating (in all senses of that word!)—"Good News" may be heard, and proclaimed.

My goal is to shock my reader—and myself, too—out of the usual habit of resisting the work of remorse. I kept "We should be ashamed of ourselves" as my first sentence because there is a real difference between the words "ashamed" and "shame," and the former word—"ashamed"—can be part of a healthy emotional response to wrongdoing. "Shame"—or more accurately, *chronic* shame—is a problematic and even neurotic response to one's own wrongdoing. Or worse, chronic shame is traumatically and abusively imposed on an innocent person by another wrongdoer. But if one merely says, "I feel ashamed," that can be a way of expressing healthy remorse, or perhaps just the first most powerful emotional experience of remorse. Beginning with "We should be ashamed of ourselves" is worth the trouble of language clarification because many people are instinctively—even actively—resistant to the topic of, and the work of, remorse, and talking about shame can help us sort out what's healthy and what's not, rather than simply resisting the whole topic altogether. Ultimately, remorse is deeply grace-filled and beneficial. Distinguishing it from chronic shame is worth the trouble.

Remorse is the task, even the calling, of the wrongdoer. Remorse is a royal road to profound grace and fullness of joy for anyone who recognizes this simple truth: "I did this thing, and I should not have done it." So many spiritual communities, so many families, so many individual lives are torn apart by unrepaired actions, by the failure of human beings to hold themselves accountable for misbehaviors both great and small. Even if forgiveness is not offered, even if it is not asked for, even if there can be no way to undo what has been done—even then, the human being bears remorse on the shield of their soul and receives from God grace upon grace. This book aims to help faith leaders whose congregants long for this grace and need only learn how to begin.

WHY REMORSE? BECAUSE OF BAD BEHAVIOR

As I said above, I was court-ordered to attend AA meetings, which began my years-long preoccupation with remorse. The first long night and day of my recovery, a day of terrible anguish, was also a day of personal resurrection.

A bit after midnight on Monday, May 13, 2013, I looked through my driver's-side window and saw a police officer beckoning me to roll down the window. I complied. I have a distinct memory of that moment: I somehow have a memory that I was parked at 6th Avenue and McGraw Street in the Queen Anne neighborhood of Seattle, a few blocks from my house. The cop wanted me to get out of the car.

My next memory was being in the police station and taking a breathalyzer test. I should say that I think I remember this. I can't be entirely sure, because the fact that I took the test, and the fact that its results (0.217) were so alarming, captured my imagination for many months after that night. I definitely remember being handcuffed in a cell at the police station, standing up, swaying, and beginning to awaken to my surroundings and my predicament. I remember too that the cell was painted a garish yellow. I was inside a bright yellow box.

My memories after that slowly came into sharper focus. *Slowly.* I was in a cab, and I wondered why we were heading south on I-5 toward Seattle. (I later learned we were traveling north.) I vaguely remember telling the cab driver how to turn onto my street on West Queen Anne. I remember paying with a credit card. (I did not yet know that I didn't have my license with me, and that I had left my checkbook open on the passenger seat of our car, which was impounded.) I remember ringing the doorbell, and I remember waiting for many minutes until my husband came to the door, let me in, and went back upstairs. I followed him upstairs, looked at the bed, and by now was fully conscious of what had happened: I had been arrested for driving under the influence, it was nearly 3:00 a.m., and I had been released on my own recognizance.

I felt a deep, staggering punch of shame. I did not want to go to bed. I remember thinking to myself that I did not deserve to sleep in our bed. I went back downstairs and passed out on the floor of my home office. I woke up sometime after 6:00 a.m. Our younger dog ran downstairs, took a quick look at me, and scampered back up to his dog bed on the main floor.

That was a wrenching day of hangover symptoms, telephone calls, and the first steps in a long journey of recovery. I hadn't remembered bringing it home with me, but the police report was on our kitchen counter. I began to read it. I discovered by reading the report that I had not been anywhere close to 6th and McGraw when I was stopped by the police. I had been on Martin Luther King Boulevard and Othello Street in south Seattle, not far from the South Precinct, where the cop had brought me to be booked. I read that the cop had stopped the field sobriety tests "for safety reasons," implying that if he had continued, I might have fallen and hurt myself. I read that I was compliant with the officer's commands. (I later reflected deeply on this compliance: I interpret it as my first truly sober behavior in my recovery, the earliest sign that God's grace was at work in me.)

I felt slight bruises—really just stress marks—on my wrists, where the handcuffs had been.

I called my bishop. I was a deacon at that point and had been for about two-and-a-half years. My bishop was compassionate and pastoral. He said, "You take care of yourself today. I mean it. *Take care of yourself.*" He talked briefly about how this could become public but was unlikely to cause much of a stir: I was a clergy person, but I wasn't a high-profile one, and to my unending, overwhelming relief, no one had been hurt. Still, it's possible that it could draw attention. If that happened, my bishop wanted me to know that I would have his support. I felt cared for in that phone call. I felt deep gratitude.

I remember spending parts of the day in the fetal position, under the covers, in bed. (I had allowed myself, in the light of day, to return to the bed.) I threw up my lunch. I made a phone call to the impound lot to be sure I knew how we could recover the car. I suspected that I should not drive, even though it was several days too early for the state department of vehicles to revoke my license. I texted my husband and asked him to take the bus down to the impound lot to get the car. When he came back with the car, I was relieved to see that it was undamaged.

I called my priest. I will never forget this call. I told her what happened and how scared and upset I was. "I love you," she said. "I love the strong parts of you, and I love the weak parts of you, and I love how they come together in one person." All these years later, this statement remains stitched on my heart. It is the statement of a pastor and theologian, a teacher and priest. It is Gospel: it is Good News.

That night I went to my first AA meeting. Days, weeks, months, years later, this day—May 13, 2013—continues to be my Day of Resurrection. This is the day I was reborn.

WHY REMORSE? BECAUSE OF DEEP RELIEF

My earliest days of sobriety were filled with fear but also tremendous relief. I was able to sleep through the night and awaken without a hangover. Even in the first couple of weeks, when resentments surged powerfully ("What am I supposed to do now?!" I whined that first Friday night, when I couldn't have a cocktail) and I was a cranky, irritable client at an outpatient rehab center, even then I couldn't help feeling *relieved*. I no longer had to drink; I was no longer going to get into trouble by drinking; I was on my way toward health.

But I was also owning up to what I had done. I told my lawyer I wanted deferred prosecution; I did not want a misdemeanor on my record. I readily admitted that I had been drunk driving (as if I could deny it!), and I agreed that if the City of Seattle gave me deferred prosecution, I would follow the requirements and suffer the consequences if I re-offended. I felt so good to simply admit that I had behaved badly.

This book is about the deep relief, the deep and joyful relief, that comes from healthy remorse. It approaches remorse with a simpler, more visceral word: *sorry*. We often feel sorry, and we just as often say (or at least should say!) "I'm sorry." But in this book we will do four things related to the word *sorry:* we will *feel* sorry, *think* sorry, *say* sorry, and *do* sorry. We "feel sorry": remorse is a feeling, or really a cluster of feelings. (One can feel sorry *for* someone, though that is a wholly different feeling and use of the word.) We "think sorry": remorse is a series of thoughts, thoughts that become a thought process and even result in a cognitive shift. In remorse we change our minds and see things (and ourselves) in a new way. We then "say sorry": remorse often (but not always) includes apologies, and at its best, those apologies are tremendously powerful and helpful to the persons we harmed. And then we "do sorry": we make amends, sometimes directly to the person we harmed, other times by living our lives in a new and better way.

As you read this book, I encourage you to notice your resistance to what you are reading and be curious about it. Like my parishioner who was upset about a Sunday-morning confession, you might find the work of remorse brings up painful memories, particularly memories of being shamed. Again, shaming someone for their misbehavior (or worse, shaming them simply because of some aspect of their identity) is directly opposed to the purpose of this book. When we do the healthy work of remorse, we fully cast aside chronic shame as the evil and abusive injury that it is. Remorse is precisely the opposite of chronic shame: when we do the work of remorse, we are participating more deeply in the grace of God, and we are employing the noblest dimensions of ourselves. Couples therapist David Schnarch, who encourages couples to focus on their best instincts and qualities, says this: "Only the best in us can talk about the worst in us, because the worst in us denies its own existence." Only the best in us can do the work of remorse, and in that work, God restores our human dignity even more wondrously than it was before we did something we should not have done. Remorse offers bountiful grace and great joy.

ACKNOWLEDGMENTS

I am thankful to many people who encouraged and supported me on this project. I begin with editor Beth Gaede, who patiently and skillfully urged me to "write from the heart," and whose many suggestions prompted my repeatedly clicking the "accept" button under each of her insightful (and helpfully bracing!) comments. I am deeply thankful to the Rev. Dr. Katherine Sonderegger, the William Meade Chair in Systematic Theology at Virginia Theological Seminary. Dr. Sonderegger is an insightful priest, a doctor of the Church, and a graceful pastor. She teaches me that every theological endeavor is prayer to, and praise of, God.

I am grateful for many other teachers and friends whose positive participation in my life—in ways sometimes large, sometimes small and subtle—informed this work: Josh

Barrett, Paul Bennett, William Boyles, Gaelen Billingsley, Zach Carstensen, Kevin Crowder, Christopher Decatur, Michael Dunckle, Claire Elser, Paul Frolick, Katherine Grieb, David Herzog, Ruthanna Hooke, Drew Jacobsen, James Joiner, Keith June, Lisa Kimball, Gordon Lathrop, Ethan Lowery, Kurt Lucks, Norine Lyons, Ian Markham, James Mathes, Florrie Munat, Alissabeth Newton, Pete Nunnally, Gail Ramshaw, Greg Rickel, Rachel Rickenbaker, Iolanthe Salant, Carrie Schofield-Broadbent, Stephen Shaver, Sam Sheridan, Melissa Skelton, Shawn Strout, Steve Thomason, Alice Torvend, Samuel Torvend, Silas Torvend, and James Urton.

I thank my father, Gary Crippen, for teaching me how to be a careful and thoughtful reader, and to bring my full intellect to the vocation of baptismal life with Christ. I thank my mother, Nancy Crippen, for teaching me our Lord's new commandment. I thank my siblings, my first and most formative companions in the work of human relationships.

Finally, my husband, Andrew, is a faithful companion, his father's son, my best friend. I am deeply grateful for his support, and for building with me a home for our small family. Thank you, Andrew. I love you.

CHAPTER 1

FEELING SORRY

In late 2015, two-and-a-half years into recovery, I flew into St. Paul, Minnesota, for my uncle's funeral. It was winter. I hadn't lived close to my dad and siblings for many years by this time—eighteen years. I was used to flying in for a few days, seeing people in a whirlwind of visits, and flying out. Like all families, we have patterns of conflict and triangulation that are tried and true. Emails were flying as various siblings planned various parts of the weekend— the funeral, the reception, and other gatherings. I began replying to emails as I was rushing around, multitasking.

One of my siblings had written a tribute to our uncle, and I was commenting on their work. I said something snarky about how it wasn't as bad as I thought it would be, "so, hey, that's a win." And then I pressed *send*. And only *then* did I realize that this sibling was on the "to" list for the email.

I panicked. I literally shuddered under a flood of adrenaline and fear. I immediately texted a couple of people on my list of "coalition siblings," the little list of siblings I am closest to. I told them I messed up, badly, and that this other sibling got my email. One of the members of my coalition called the sibling I had hurt and talked over what happened (part of the triangulation pattern in our family). But I knew I had to do something. I had to be direct and call the sibling myself and apologize. And that's it—just an apology. No appeal for forgiveness, no excuses. I recalled Step 10 in AA, which says we "continued to take personal inventory, and when we were wrong, promptly admitted it." I knew what I had to do.

I made the call and said I was sorry. "I am really sorry, I really am," I said. "There's no excuse for what I did. I was being snarky and insensitive, and you didn't deserve that." I listened as the sibling told me their experience of my email, in a somewhat broken voice. They said that they were hurt in part because they have a long history of writing, and writing well, and were shocked that someone in the family would so blithely make fun of their writing. And it also hurt because they too were close to our uncle, arguably closer than most of us, not that this sibling was asserting that!

I apologized again. I said I wanted to do anything I could to make things right. My sibling was gracious and said that it was enough that we talked about it, and we agreed to move on. As the rest of the weekend went by, we talked, a little stiffly, but in a friendly way. The problem was resolved.

I felt better. *Much better.* I had done Step 10 with my sibling: "We continued to take personal inventory, and when we were wrong, promptly admitted it." I flew home feeling that I had not behaved well over the weekend, but that I had at least made repairs for my bad behavior. I often return to this story, years later, with chagrin, but also with a deeper sense of satisfaction that what was broken was repaired.

Stories like this, with all the feelings that freight them, are often what we think of when we hear the word remorse. I felt ashamed. I felt anxious. I felt angry (with myself). I felt nervous and edgy. I felt sorrow, sadness, even anguish. But I felt *relief*, too, once I came clean and had the conversation I needed to have. I felt no small amount of satisfaction that I had started that conversation and didn't need to be pulled into it or yanked into it. All these feelings! But some of them are good!

THE BITTERNESS AND BLESSINGS OF REMORSE

Remorse is a collection of feelings, thoughts, and behaviors, but we begin with feelings: remorse is *feeling* sorry. It is an emotional experience. We might not want to ask our congregants to recite the confession on Sundays or to reflect on amends they need to make to someone they have harmed. We might prefer talking about how God loves us and God's grace is found abundantly around and within us. And these are true things! God does love us! God's grace is around and within us! But God's grace is also powerful enough to change and heal us, especially when we confront our own wrongdoing. God loves me and showers grace upon me whether or not I call my sibling and apologize, and whether or not I get sober and make amends following a DUI arrest. But God's love and grace is ever more real for me, and works ever more deeply within me, when I feel the hard feelings of remorse and reflect, with God's help, on those feelings. Either way, God does not change. But if I face these feelings, I then receive the blessing that follows them.

PETER AT THE CAMPFIRE

In Luke 22, Peter denies Jesus. Luke, that great storyteller, sketches a scene in which Jesus is moving from one place to another and passes through the little courtyard where Peter huddles by a thin, dying fire, trying in vain to get warm. Then his Lord walks by and simply looks at him. No words. No commentary. No raised finger in accusation. None of that is needed, because both Jesus and Peter know what happened. Jesus had even predicted it. Jesus simply looks at Peter, and Peter fully recognizes what he has done. And then his *feelings* descend on him. In Luke's telling, Peter walks away, "weeping bitterly."

To his credit, Peter does not chase after Jesus in a pathetic attempt to repair the damage. He does his victim the courtesy of removing himself from the scene. He saves his weeping for his own company, his own time. Maybe Jesus wasn't available anyway because he was essentially on a "perp walk," moving toward the next phase of his trial ahead of his execution. But I like to think that Peter had the opportunity to bother Jesus, to run up to him and plead for mercy and forgiveness, and chose not to do that. His choice can be read as a small but sure sign of dignity and fortitude in Peter's character.

Still, Peter had a lot of weeping to do. *Bitter* weeping at that. He goes on to be not only an apostle, but the chief apostle, preaching a stirring Resurrection sermon to the Jerusalem authorities in Luke's second volume, the Acts of the Apostles. Peter dies a martyr's death—the death of a witness to the Good News of Jesus Christ. He lends his name to some of the most august fortresses in Christian architecture. He is an inspiration to millions. But before all of that, on that night, Peter was lost in his terrible feelings. He wept bitterly. He knew what he had done, and on that most awful night, all he could do was weep—alone.

As painful as remorse often is, the feelings can also be blessings or gifts. They do serve as helpful motivators, and they also signify that God's grace is already at work in us, even before we have pursued reconciliation with the person we harmed or amended our lives. When we feel sorry for what we have done, the grace of remorse has begun its work in, with, and through us.

ST. ANSELM'S PENITENCE

Peter simply "went away, weeping bitterly," but a thousand years later Anselm of Canterbury expressed as part of his private prayers awful feelings of remorse with vivid and wrenching detail. While we understandably want to avoid these feelings, not even wishing to talk about them, we may find some insight and even comfort in the devotional life of St. Anselm. Anselm plunges deeply into the bitterness of remorse in one of his prayers to Mary, the mother of Jesus: "Horrible fear, terrible grief, inconsolable sorrow, heap yourselves upon me, rush upon me, overwhelm me, confuse, cover, possess me. It is just, it is just. With shameless audacity I have despised you, by shameless delights I have provoked you; nay, rather God, not you: and now in miserable penitence I long for you."[1]

"Miserable penitence" is not the speed of most people today. We don't come to church to feel miserable, and we tend to look for the exit the moment we sense that a church is about to take us in that direction. Even when someone is in the throes of emotional remorse, lost in their anguished feelings, they rarely think or feel that anything good, let alone joyful, could be awaiting them if they would only face those feelings and let those feelings have their say. The grief of poor Anselm, praying in near despair, may even ring in our ears as overblown, absurd. But he shows us that authentic self-confrontation lifts a burden and allows a person to rest. He does this by expressing his anguish as a vital part of his prayer life.

In the days after I got sober in May 2013, I was filled with remorse about my foolishness, my wasteful and self-indulgent behaviors in the last days and weeks of my drinking life. I didn't kill anyone; I didn't even kill my marriage (though perhaps I came close a couple of times). But I did put other people at risk, and I mistreated many people—family, friends, co-workers, neighbors. I was sick, yes; but I was also culpable.

In the first few days of sobriety, when I was physically sobering up, I had post-acute withdrawal syndrome—PAWS, the shakes, which many people newly in recovery experience. But my emotions also caused physical shaking, shortness of breath, and a deepening dread about the full impact of my actions, much of which still lay ahead. Years later, reading Anselm, I felt a connection. Anselm's prayer may sound antiquated and even pathetic to our ears. But I sensed that I understood how he was feeling, even if we lived a full millennium apart from one another. I recognized and empathized with his anguish. What's more, I found it appropriate to focus on these feelings as part of my spiritual work.

In my own experience, even in the earliest days of my recovery, the blessings appeared quickly. I was finally able to sleep, to deeply rest, and to awaken refreshed. Yes, I was emotionally distraught, more than I had been before or have been since. I had been charged with driving under the influence, and I was facing (among other things) the requirement to install a breathalyzer in our car for a year (my husband's and mine—he too would have to breathe into the device to start our car). This reinforced my self-centered anguish about my bad behaviors. *But I slept!*

I was no longer drinking, and so physically my body was able to actually sleep. Yes, I would awaken with many fears, but I would also awaken without a hangover. And yet it wasn't just the physical absence of alcohol that improved my sleep. It was also the knowledge that I was finally facing up to what I had done, and I was beginning to hold myself accountable for it. I was beginning to work with my feelings, including and especially my feeling sorry.

I did not find in Anselm's writings the joyful side of remorse that I myself have experienced. But I wonder if (and hope that) he slept well, enjoying restful slumber because, in exploring his true feelings, he was being honest, authentic, with himself and with God. "No rest for the wicked," goes the old cliché, but there is rest for the remorseful. I hope for his sake that he did find that gladness. Whether he did or not, though, we learn from him that, in remorse, we can pray. Anselm prayed through and with his awful feelings, readily naming and expressing them. I also did this, though I didn't have Anselm's spiritual discipline, so I did not turn first to St. Mary or to God: I confided in my lawyer. I sat in a chair in my home office, my lawyer sitting opposite me, quietly going over her intake paperwork with me. She seemed utterly unperturbed by me or my story, while I sat in my chair literally trembling with fear and remorse. I said to her, simply, "I'm just so scared."

"I know," she said, "but you'll get through this." She may have even said something bracing like, "Many people are far worse off than you. Many people have done more terrible things than you. And yes, many people have also *not* done the things you did, and so they aren't sitting in that chair feeling scared and alone. So you're somewhere in the broad middle. You're a human who messed up. Don't worry. You'll be okay. You'll fix it." No, she definitely didn't say all of that. But in my conversation with her, I believe someone (or Someone) said that to me. It began to dawn on me: I was going to be okay. But that dawning happened in the midst of my awful feelings of remorse.

Meanwhile, I returned to church, serving as an Episcopal deacon. I prayed with my faith community. I also began outpatient treatment, and while their methods were nonsectarian and cognitive-behavioral, they also employed the twelve-step prayers (and the Twelve Steps themselves) as part of their treatment design, and we routinely said the Serenity Prayer and the Set-Aside Prayer, a prayer in which we ask God to help us set aside everything we think we know about ourselves, our illness, and God, so that we might learn something new. And finally, I attended AA meetings, where the Serenity Prayer was said each time. In all these contexts, I said my prayers alongside confessions of wrongdoing and many hard feelings of remorse.

I began to make progress. It all felt (and still feels) grace-filled, nourishing, and deeply relieving.

OTHER PERSPECTIVES

Even as we work hard, as I did, to *do sorry* (more on this in chapter 4), the blessing of remorse can be difficult to recognize. Episcopal priest Robert Francis Capon, in his book *The Mystery of Christ, and Why We Don't Get It*, even seems to suggest that remorse is contrary to the Gospel. Capon introduces his readers to "Helen," a parishioner (or perhaps a composite of parishioners) who comes to him with a dilemma: she wants to continue pursuing a romantic relationship outside of her marriage, but she is aware that this may be the wrong thing to do. She assumes that her priest will advise her to end the affair, and she already has difficult feelings of regret. Capon disarms her with his counsel, however. He tells her he believes she already knows what she wants to do and can probably predict for herself what she in fact *will* do. And he adds that, whatever her decision, God will forgive her. Indeed, God already has forgiven her:

In Jesus' death and resurrection, the whole test-passing, brownie-point-earning rigmarole of the human race has been canceled for lack of interest on God's part. All he needs from us is a simple Yes or No, and off to work he goes. If we say Yes to something wrong, or No to something right, he will reconcile it all by himself. Not only *can* he handle it, he's *already* handled it: he has all our messes fixed in Jesus—right now, even before we make them. All we have to do is trust his assurance that losers are his cup of tea.[2]

Capon goes on to dismiss as irrelevant the remorseful feelings his parishioners sometimes report. "The premise of my counsel to Helen was just this," he wrote: *"the guilt shop has been closed*, boarded up entirely and for good by God's grace and nothing else."[3] He wants his parishioner to do her ethical discernment free of any pressure from a judging or convicting god, her way forward alight with the bright Good News of the saving love of God in Jesus, who has already forgiven her, no matter what she does.

But Capon, in his dismissal of guilt as an unhelpful spiritual condition, overlooks the power and gift of remorse. God forgives our sins, but God also stirs our conscience through the Spirit; our remorse is evidence of God at work in us. Because this remorse is a gift of God, it is not wasteful, or self-abusive, or (as in Capon's framework) a heretical lack of faith in the Gospel.

In contrast, the Episcopal theologian Fleming Rutledge reflects on the feelings attendant to remorse and how, as awful as they are, they lead to a particularly intense experience of joyful relief—bitterness and blessing. For her, the music of J. S. Bach illustrates how remorse is a powerful—if painful—gift:

> In Bach's music, the knowledge of sin is encompassed by rapturous gladness. Bach's unique contribution to the church's worship is the way he frequently combines passages of the deepest anguish with dance forms and their capacity for inspiring delight. . . . Part of the effectiveness of the music at these points is Bach's affinity for Martin Luther's experience of *Anfechtung*—a soul-threatening attack. This will help us understand how a knowledge of sin, a sense of estrangement, and all other manifestations of *Anfechtung*, when understood *from within the context of saving grace*, bring an unburdened happiness to the human heart."[4]

If we can identify with Peter huddled around the campfire and with Anselm in fervent prayer, overcome with anguish about his wrongdoing, we may finally see that Jesus's terrible (if merciful) look stirs our conscience helpfully, even creatively, in God-given remorse, with all of its attendant awful feelings, and with the piercing joy that awaits us when we contemplate what we have done in the light of God's grace. Human remorse does not save human souls from damnation—an old, abusive, and harmful idea that was meant to scare people into confessing their sins under the threat of hell. But remorse is nonetheless a gift of God, who in the saving work of the Redeemer draws even wretched traitors into a shared consciousness of both human wrongdoing and divine grace.

CORPORATE REMORSE

Whole communities, and not just individuals, can experience the bitterness and blessing of remorse. We can easily make the mistake, in our reflections on Peter and Anselm, of focusing on them as individuals whose stories offer meaning only to themselves. It may even be self-centered to imagine oneself as a solitary remorseful person. But one is never alone in the effort to find warmth and light by the dim embers of Peter's campfire or in Anselm's solemn prayer room. Christians are guilty of shared wrongdoing, acts both done and undone, and are called to corporate confession.

Sunday by Sunday, many Christians recite a corporate confession of sins. "Let us confess our sins against God and our neighbor," the Episcopal deacon intones. The plural personal pronoun in this confession is significant: *We* have sinned against God. But corporate confession is complicated. Some members of the assembly may be far less culpable than others (consider a spouse confessing her participation in corporate sin while standing next to her abuser). Not everyone uses their privileges to hurt others. Some congregants (perhaps most!) may not understand why we confess sins corporately. But at its best, the corporate confession of sins is a way for the gathered Christian community to enter together into the painful feelings of remorse, for any sins committed by the individuals gathered in the room together, but also for wrongdoing for which the whole community truly shares responsibility. The Episcopal Church's *Sacred Ground* curriculum offers a major example of corporate sin: the curriculum of films, readings, and guided discussions leads groups of people with white privilege to acknowledge their shared participation in white supremacy and institutional racism. This corporate work helps participants move beyond unhelpful personal shame and defensiveness and leads the larger community into productive antiracism work.

WORKING WITH FEELINGS

Sometimes, when working with feelings, we need to understand them at a basic level. What is a "feeling"? What's a good word for it? How do I know how I feel, unless I can understand better what feelings are in the first place?

"Mad, sad, glad, afraid." These are often what people think of when they think about feelings. "Mad, sad, glad, and afraid" are the four "food groups" of feelings, the four categories, the four big names for umpteen feelings: "boredom" goes in the sadness column because it's a mild form of depression; "agitated" goes in the afraid column because it is a mild form of anxiety. (Or is "agitated" a form of anger? Perhaps! The four categories are useful ways to sort through and identify feelings, but these are not hard scientific constructs.)

Therapists routinely help clients process their feelings, yet many of us step into church and readily suppress or deny our harder feelings, often with the church's encouragement. We push anger below the surface and express it almost exclusively in passive-aggressive behaviors or by "voting with our feet": we simply leave church when we (or others) get angry. The expression of sadness also fares poorly in many churches. There are few "Our Lady of Sorrows" churches anymore. Few congregations would appreciate the church on Jerusalem's Mount of Olives that is shaped like a teardrop because it is at that location that pilgrims believe Jesus stood when he gazed at the city and wept. "Oh Jerusalem, Jerusalem!" Jesus cried, perhaps from that very overlook. "How often have I desired to gather your children together as a hen gathers her brood under her wings, and you were not willing!" (Luke 13:34). For many churches, this lament of Jesus is simply too sad.

Guilt and shame, though, are the true pariahs among feelings. Faith leaders may avoid these to the point that they forget to explain to their congregants the difference between them. Guilt is an emotion, as well as a finding in jurisprudence. It is the emotion I feel when I realize I did something wrong: I feel guilty. Shame is not the same emotional experience as guilt, however, and if we distinguish them, we can set shame aside and work on guilt, the emotional dimension of remorse. If a parishioner feels guilty because they did something wrong, does your faith community talk about guilt? Are you afraid that discussing these problems will feel unwelcoming or judgmental, and that your congregants will feel shamed, ridiculed, or rejected—by your community or by God? Or do you deal with guilt directly, reassuring people that not only is the feeling common, it is actually sometimes useful and can even lead to the joyful relief of remorse in the context of God's grace?

I wrote earlier that when I began to realize that I had been arrested for drunk driving, I felt "a staggering punch of shame." I can't think of a better way to describe the feeling in that moment, but it was only that—a moment. That "punch of shame" was followed by guilty feelings, feelings that proved to be part of a healthy experience of remorse. But the "shame" that is different from guilt is this: it is a chronic negative self-judgment that becomes self-abusive. (Often enough, chronic shame is imposed upon a person by an abuser, or in an abusive family pattern.) When I am feeling chronic shame of this kind, I am moving beyond the simple emotion of (healthy) guilt and making a negative (and neurotic) self-judgment on the evidence of my wrongdoing. I drove while intoxicated. I am guilty of this. But this is not evidence that I am a bad person. Shame, unlike guilt, is both unproductive and abusive. It adds nothing constructive to a human life, but it does do real damage to a human life.

In the first forty days of my recovery, I slowly began to learn the difference between guilt and shame. I recall the number of days because when I returned to church, I decided not to receive Holy Communion for forty days. I followed the ancient Lenten practice in which those who were guilty of notorious sins would spend time out of communion with the larger community during Lent and be restored and forgiven at Easter. I mentioned this to one of my friends—another churchgoer who was in formation for the priesthood—and he looked at me, frowned, and said with bracing good humor, "Would you just get over yourself and get in line for Communion with the rest of us sinners?" His gruff but kind-hearted rebuke reminded me that attending church—and perhaps especially getting in line for Communion—are behaviors that guilty people do, and that only shame would prevent me from participating as a full and equal member of the community. If I am working through healthy (if hard) feelings of guilt, then the Word and sacraments are there for my benefit—blessing follows bitterness—just as they are for everyone else. And if I am laboring under unhealthy feelings of shame, then those same means of grace are even more powerfully there to relieve me of chronic shame and welcome me with everyone else in corporate confession and forgiveness, each one of us lovely in God's sight.

Sister Helen Prejean can help us distinguish guilt from shame. She counsels and advocates for inmates on death row, helping them admit what they did wrong and to recognize it as the wrong thing to do. She is not shaming them! Not even a convicted murderer should descend into a "shame spiral," as the experience of shame is sometimes called.

Now, if my actions ever did lead to the death of a human being, I expect I would feel a tremendous amount of chronic shame. (I was arrested while driving only five miles an hour in a deserted area, and just doing that led me to experience that punch of shame!) But again, chronic shame is at best worthless, and it usually causes further damage, in this case to the wrongdoer. Rather than working with healthy guilt to confess wrongdoing and make amends, the wrongdoer, when lost in shame, becomes self-focused and preoccupied with a distorted and negative self-image. This is corrosive and unhelpful. The wrongdoer is, like their victims, a human being. Nothing destructive or abusive of any human being should be endorsed or encouraged. Churches should stay out of the shame business. But church members and leaders should nevertheless confront the shame their congregants feel (my friend's rebuke of my withdrawal from Communion is a good example of confronting shame). They should respond to the guilt their congregants are working on by inviting them into individual and corporate practices of confession, amends, and forgiveness, beginning with a pastoral and empathetic embrace of their healthy, if painful, feelings of remorse.

I am a priest, and before that I was a psychotherapist. I have spent many hours trying to help people move beyond their shame. Churches can and should do this. God loves all creation, so of course God loves all people. God does not want people to be victims of shame, inflicted by the self or by others. "You are precious in my sight and honored and I love you," God says in Isaiah 43:4, and in Ezekiel 18:23 God asks rhetorically, "Have I any pleasure in the death of the wicked . . . and not rather that they should turn from their ways and live?"

Still, as a priest, I have wanted to spend more time talking about guilt than I have sensed anyone wants me to do; I have wanted to lead congregants more deeply into the work of confession; I have wanted to show people that there is deep grace and profound joy to be had in doing this guilt work. But there seems to be resistance all around.

Here is a way to begin talking about guilt and shame in your congregation:

1. Preach and talk with people about the difference between guilt and shame. Stress that they are essentially different emotional states and that only one of them is useful. Proclaim the Good News that God does not shame human beings.

2. Talk about guilt in ways that are disarming and invitational. Encourage discernment (individually and in groups) that focuses on wrongdoing as a healthy topic, scary as it may be.

3. In preaching, small-group discussion, and individual work with parishioners, read and reflect on stories from Scripture and our tradition that address guilt. Facilitate questions, objections, and wonderings about these stories. Helpful biblical passages for reflection on remorse include the following. (This is not an exhaustive list!)

A. Genesis 4:1–16: Cain kills his brother Abel in this primeval story.

B. Genesis 32–33: Jacob is afraid of his brother, whom he had hurt and betrayed; he wrestles with a divine stranger and reconciles with his brother.

C. Genesis 37–50: The story of Joseph and his brothers and their prolonged reconciliation, a novella, closes the book of Genesis.

D. 2 Samuel 11–12: The prophet Nathan confronts King David about his great sin, and David repents.

E. Psalm 51: This song of remorse ends with God's promise of restoration.

F. Lamentations 1: A poet expresses remorse about the desolate city of Jerusalem.

G. Matthew 27:3–5, Acts 1:18–19: Judas dies, and the differing accounts of his death offer insights about remorse (and perhaps its devastating absence).

H. Luke 15:11–32: In the parable of the Lost Son(s), the younger son is in touch with his own guilt; the older son is not and wants to shame his younger brother. Both sons are welcome at the feast.

I. John 8:1–11: Jesus responds to the guilty men who are scapegoating a woman.

THOUGHTS AND FEELINGS

A few days after my arrest, I sat in one of the black barrel chairs in my own therapy office, one of the chairs my clients normally sat in, while my lawyer looked down at her paperwork and made notes, preparing to coach me on what was coming next. I was trembling, deeply frightened, powerfully unnerved, scared literally out of my wits: I couldn't think clearly. I finally began to think about my dad, who spent his career working as a county-court and state-appellate judge: I was the first child of his to get arrested. This thought about my father—a thought, not a feeling—provides a bridge to the next chapter, when we will set feelings aside and focus on the thoughts that attend authentic remorse. Both feelings and thoughts need to be treated, the feelings dispelled and the thoughts corrected. For me, the time would come for that. But there, in that office chair, perhaps it was good that I was in the throes of my feelings. The music of Bach could have accompanied my anguish; pastors could have drawn alongside me to minister to me and even hear my confession. On that day, my sole human companion was my good, kind, and matter-of-fact lawyer, who simply presented calm confidence while I trembled in fear and mortification. I prayed first to her and then, more directly, to God: "Can you help me?" I asked her. "Of course," she said, thoroughly unruffled by the emotional havoc I was experiencing. "Oh, help," I would pray to God, again and again, in the following months.

I felt sorry. That was a healthy first step in my recovery, and in my reconciliation with myself, with others, and with God.

CHAPTER 2

THINKING SORRY

In 2016, I decided I wanted to work the Twelve Steps again. I found a new sponsor, and we began the process together. He came to my home, a key difference from the first time I worked the Steps, when I drove to my then-sponsor's home. In retrospect, I think there was something valuable in my driving to the sponsor, rather than the sponsor driving to me: this is my work, not the sponsor's.

We would sit down in my home office, on the lower level, where I saw clients as a psychotherapist and where I had first collapsed in guilt and shame on my first day of sobriety. I chose to sit in the chair normally used by my clients to remind myself that if the roles weren't exactly reversed, they were certainly *different* from those of my therapy sessions.

My new sponsor was a bit more gruff, direct, and straightforward than my first one. He was less genial, more businesslike. He was also gay, like me. I liked the difference because I felt as if another gay man might have a stronger bullshit detector for certain in-group things. And I was right.

I began my new work by moving through Steps 1 through 3. Only Step 1, in which the person admits their powerlessness over alcohol, mentions the substance, a fact you're sure to hear at an AA meeting if you attend enough times. The subject of the Twelve Steps is not alcohol: it is one's own ledger, one's own "side of the street," and how only a "higher power" can help the alcoholic truly enter recovery and stay in it. In the first three steps, the recovering alcoholic turns toward their higher power for help. Then, in Steps 4 through 9, the recovering alcoholic, always with the help of their higher power, makes a thorough inventory of the things they have done or not done that require amends, and begins the process of amends. Finally, in Steps 10 through 12, the recovering alcoholic pursues a new pattern of spiritual living that applies these steps, deepens spiritual awareness, and shares the message with other alcoholics.

Step 3 was interesting this second time I moved through the steps. My new sponsor wasn't Christian. He knew I was a faith leader in Christian churches, though, so he moved quickly to prevent me from misunderstanding the concept, and the point, of a higher power. "Stay out of the Sistine Chapel," I recall him saying, though I can't be sure he actually said that. I may have said that to myself as he described the exercise. He wanted me to imagine a higher power that works, or fits, for me alone. Imagine someone or something that resonates with you, he suggested. Is there a person, or a group of people, or an animal, or an ocean, or something—anything—that you can turn to and hand over control of your illness?

I thought of someone: Audrey Hepburn in the film *Always*. I remember she was wearing a white sweater. She was an otherworldly being, an angel, perhaps. She met Richard Dreyfuss in the afterlife and served as his guide. When I told my new sponsor Audrey Hepburn was my higher power, he said in perfect deadpan, "That's pretty gay." I accepted that as a sign that I had completed my assignment. I was now to imagine Audrey Hepburn—or *Hap*, the name of her character in *Always*—when I worked with my higher power in the Steps.

Then it was time for Step 4, in which I do my own moral inventory. I began by making a list of my resentments, and my new sponsor quickly pushed me to dig deep into the resentments I had about one person in particular. This was a friend who stopped being my friend and did so in a way that was deeply painful for me (and, of course, heavily complicated by my own problematic actions). I'm not overstating things to say that our conflict and falling out traumatized me. I included this person in my list (and in my prayers) and wrote in a few others.

I no longer have the list. That, too, is significantly different from the first time I worked through the steps. My first journey through them is meticulously recorded and included in my overstuffed white recovery binder, the one that includes the police report from my DUI and my AA attendance slips. It would have been a good idea to include these notes in the binder too: throughout my recovery, I have meticulously documented the intentional things I've done to recover, from the paper stack of court-ordered AA-meeting slips to the hundreds of runs I've recorded on a fitness app. The fact that I didn't keep my second Step-4 list suggests that I wasn't truly working the steps this time.

When it came time to do Step 5 ("[We] admitted to God, to ourselves, and to another human being the exact nature of our wrongs"), my new sponsor came to my home again, and we settled in my office. I began telling him about my Step-4 list. We weren't long into my narrative when he stopped me and asked me to go back. He noticed that I had admitted a big mistake that I hadn't talked about in our previous conversations. It was big enough that I really should have disclosed it far earlier. It wasn't that I had relapsed on alcohol and hadn't told him, but it seemed that big. My silence sent the message to my sponsor that I hadn't been honest with him from the start.

He asked me directly if I really wanted to do the Steps right now. He was right to ask this. I wasn't ready. More honestly, I didn't want to. I wasn't ready to step away from some of the patterns of interaction that kept me locked in resentment.

This sounds like a feelings story, but it truly is a good introduction to our reflections on the cognitive dimensions of remorse. Feelings and thoughts go together. They inform each other. But Steps 4 and 5 guide the recovering alcoholic in pulling them apart. For example, I felt fear and anger about my friend's abandonment of me, but in the fourth step I pushed past those feelings (or through them) to identify the thought errors that led to the hard feelings. My second trip through the Twelve Steps was full of feelings, but as I worked the Step, I discovered it wasn't the feelings that were tripping me up. It was the thought errors. I still wasn't ready to think clearly about friendships and other parts of my life that kept me in a "dry drunk" and held me back in my recovery. (A "dry drunk" is not actively abusing a substance but is still behaving in other problematic, pre-recovery ways.) For example, I harbored the thought error that the friend who hurt me was obligated not to hurt me. This is an understandable thought, but it is not true: others are free to behave—and misbehave—as they choose. I need not be in relationship with those who behave hurtfully, but they are free individuals. In AA parlance, although I wasn't relapsing on alcohol, my thought errors were moving me closer to my next drink, rather than further away.

I honestly don't remember exactly how my sponsor and I ended our relationship. I know I didn't make it past Step 5. He ended that meeting (fairly amicably), and we may have met again, at least once. We stayed connected on social media. At some point he added me to his Christmas-card list. (I felt relieved about this: I liked him and was glad that he stayed friends with me.) There were of course no hard feelings: this is my life, and he had been my sponsor as part of his own recovery story. If I ended up not being a long-term sponsee, that was not a problem for him; he could always help somebody else.

But I felt a lingering regret. I had not done the cognitive work, the work of correcting thought errors and making conscious choices to behave better. I had not been fully honest with myself, with God, or with my new sponsor. As I write this, years later, I still have not relapsed on alcohol, and I am in a much better emotional *and* cognitive place than I was back then. Still, I missed an opportunity. I could have worked harder: I could have worked the steps more honestly and with more commitment and intention.

CHANGING HOW WE THINK

So, yes, remorse is about feelings. But it is more than mere feelings, and lousy feelings at that. Remorse is a *stance*, a particular way of looking at one's own behavior. Remorse is spiritual work that engages our minds, our intellects, our intelligence. Remorse empowers a person to stand taller, to see farther, to breathe more deeply, even to rejoice in wisdom. For all of that to happen, we must think differently about our actions.

Philosopher John Perry, who has taught at both Stanford and the University of California, offers a homely but memorable image for this turn of mind: "I once followed a trail of sugar on a supermarket floor, pushing my cart down the aisle on one side of a tall counter and back up the aisle on the other, seeking the shopper with the torn sack to tell him he was making a mess. With each trip around the counter, the trail became thicker. But I seemed unable to catch up. Finally, it dawned on me. I was the shopper I was trying to catch."[1]

For Perry, when the shopper says, "*I* am making a mess," they are changing their thinking about the situation. In the old way of thinking, the wrongdoing was done by someone else, and the shopper sat in judgment of the wrongdoer. After shifting to the thought, "I am making a mess," the shopper self-identifies as the wrongdoer. It is one thing to look around and form opinions about what has gone wrong in the world: a polluted watershed here, a misleading column of yellow journalism there. From a small, grim, and impatient conflict on a subway car to the atrocity of genocide, there is much wrongdoing to behold. Perry's shift in thinking is simply the realization, "*I* have done this." Or as the old hymn has it, more sharply and disturbingly, "I crucified thee."[2] This shift alone is a powerful and necessary component of healthy remorse.

Note that we are focusing here not on the feelings of remorse, but on the thoughts. This is a change in consciousness, a cognitive recognition, an insight. *I* am responsible for this polluted waterway. *I* keep quiet while journalists spread false information. *I* did nothing to intervene or prevent a personal altercation on the subway. *I* am partially responsible for my culture's indifference to genocide.

Stories and insights from scripture can illumine this point. In Genesis, just after Adam and Eve have eaten from the tree, God walks through the garden at the time of the evening breeze, calling out to them, "Where are you?" *Where are you?*—"thinking sorry" is recognizing and admitting where we are. When I think to myself, "I have done this thing, and I was wrong to do it," I am orienting myself toward God. I am turning my head in God's direction, as God walks through the garden in the evening. I am changing my mind and beginning to look at my own behavior as God does—not with disgust or shame (again, this is about the *thinking* dimension of remorse), but with a basic yet powerful cognitive shift. "I am guilty. I did it." Remorse is an orientation to God, a turning of one's moral compass in the direction of God's mercy, surely, but also and especially God's judgment.

The Bible of course has many more stories that illuminate the cognitive shift of remorse. King David is remembered for his remorse following Nathan's brave confrontation of the monarch with the truth of his terrible wrongdoing: David's decision to take Bathsheba into his own bed, and then have her husband murdered. Nathan begins indirectly but then confronts the king bluntly: "You are that man." We remember David's anguish, and each Ash Wednesday we sing the psalm that likely expresses that anguish, Psalm 51. But when we explore the psalm, we may also see, alongside but distinct from the emotional agony, that simple change of mind discussed above by John Perry. "I have done what is evil in your sight," David (or the psalmist through whom we hear David) sings, simply. While there is great and painful feeling in these psalm verses, there is also an almost ordinary self-examination. It was me. I did it.

THE POWER OF THINKING SORRY

The personal history of a remarkable woman can illumine for us the power of "thinking sorry." Helen Prejean, CSJ, a Catholic religious leader in the Congregation of the Sisters of St. Joseph, builds close relationships with death-row inmates, innocent and guilty alike, and she has an admirable gift for seeing the humanity in the worst offenders. A key dimension of Helen's ministry is her ability to connect her own history of wrongdoing to the bad (albeit significantly worse!) behavior of the inmates she counsels.

In the film about Sister Prejean, *Dead Man Walking*, we meet Helen as a young girl in a series of flashbacks. We see her happily undergoing a religious ceremony, her admittance to the Sisters of Saint Joseph of Medaille, in 1957 at the age of eighteen. But as she begins to build a relationship with death-row inmate Matthew Poncelet, we are taken back further to a time when, as a younger girl, Helen participated with her playmates in the brutal beating and killing of a possum. Still haunted by this early experience, Helen approaches Matthew with empathy. Perhaps she—perhaps each of us—has something in common with this human being whom many throughout the film call "a monster," "scum," a "mad dog." "It's easy to kill a monster," says Hilton Barber, an attorney Helen retains to offer *pro bono* legal help to Matthew. It is less easy to kill someone whose horrible behavior has even a small parallel with the everyday cruelty of ordinary human children.

Note the cognitive connection Helen makes between her own history and the actions of the inmate. She is haunted by her own wrongdoing, experiencing its emotional consequences many years later. But the connection she draws is a straightforward, logical one: I also have the capacity for cruelty, Helen reasons. Therefore, I can understand the convict in front of me, and I have the capacity to assist him.

A good fictional example of remorse as a shift in thinking, a move from deflection toward recognition of personal culpability, can be seen in the television drama *The West Wing*. President Jed Bartlet is telling a close advisor why he has chosen to accept Congress's censure of his behavior. He says to the advisor:

I was wrong. I was. I was just ... *I was wrong.* Come on, you know that. Lots of times we don't know what right or wrong is but lots of times we do and come on, this is one. I may not have had sinister intent at the outset but there were plenty of opportunities for me to make it right. No one in government takes responsibility for anything anymore. We foster, we obfuscate, we rationalize. "Everybody does it." That's what we say. So we come to occupy a moral safe house where everyone's to blame so no one's guilty. I'm to blame. I was wrong.[3]

The president faced congressional censure for lying to the American public about his own degenerative illness, multiple sclerosis. In this episode, his advisors are discerning how best to politically survive this scandal of the president's own making, preferably by avoiding his own personal responsibility for the crisis. The president likely could have survived the fallout of his decision to conceal his illness: he was bright, politically skillful, and admired as an ethical and principled leader. He plausibly could have made his case to the American people that he did nothing wrong, that perhaps his decision to hide his condition was unwise or even upsetting, but it was nonetheless reasonable and eminently understandable. But he knew the public would suffer noticeable damage if he attempted to excuse his behavior. They would no longer enjoy easy confidence in the probity of their leaders. They would not experience the satisfaction of an authentic apology for behavior that denied them their right to elect their leader with all relevant information about the candidates. The nation would proceed diminished. He came to believe that if he simply admitted he was wrong not to disclose his health issue, if he apologized and accepted the judgment of his peers, then the electorate would be strengthened. Honor would be restored to the public square. True repair could be made. Jed's changing his thinking made this possible.

HOW TO DO IT

In all of these examples—God confronting the human ones in the garden, Nathan challenging the monarch to hold himself accountable, a nun helping death-row inmates admit their guilt, and a president owning up to his own mistake—we may be enlightened and even inspired by the changes of both mind and heart the characters experience. But how do we do it? How do we begin to "think sorry"?

In the rite for the Reconciliation of a Penitent in the Episcopal *Book of Common Prayer*, Form One,[4] the priest concludes the rite by saying to the penitent, "Go (or abide) in peace, and pray for me, a sinner." This is a surprising turn in the rite: the priest acknowledges to the person who just confessed their sins that she—the priest—*also* needs to confess sins. The rite also provides time for the priest to counsel the penitent, suggesting various things they can do as part of their work of remorse. This rite reveals beautifully how all members of a congregation—including the pastor—are called to work individually and together on this work.

Here are two possible ways to begin talking about "thinking sorry" in your congregation, beyond the formal encounter of an individual rite of reconciliation.

1. Select stories about remorse from Scripture, popular culture, art, and literature, and read them together, taking time for reflection and perhaps even close study. Then encourage congregants to tell their own stories of remorse, and share your own, as appropriate. Recalling John Perry's story of the remorseful shopper, facilitate the group's reflection on the *thoughts* they have about the behaviors they regret: How do they make sense of

what happened? What thought errors (for example, "I'm a bad person because I did that") have they struggled with?

Certain stories from our faith tradition may help them shift their thinking in a more helpful direction. For example, in the closing chapters of Genesis, we read the story of the reconciliation of Joseph and his eleven brothers. In that long, eventful, and emotionally complicated section of Genesis, it can be hard to see how various characters changed their minds and thought about their own behavior in new ways. The brother Judah stands out: he realizes his own mistakes (and those of his brothers) and proves himself faithful to Joseph, empowering Joseph to reconcile with the brothers who had harmed him so badly. Your group could read this story together and reflect on their own experiences of thinking differently about a painful conflict, holding themselves accountable, and allowing that change in thinking to guide them into new and healthier actions.

2. Encourage individuals to work alone, or one-on-one with you or a trusted friend, on mapping out (note the cognitive flavor of that image!) their own "ledger," their own "side of the street." Was there

something they did, or something they did not do, that they regret? What was it about that behavior that they themselves recognize to be a problem? And what are their thoughts about that behavior?

This of course is the work of Steps 4 and 5 in Alcoholics Anonymous, and those materials are widely available for people to consider and use. But the field of cognitive behavioral therapy also offers many resources for this cognitive work. Consider making use of a cognitive behavioral therapy "thought record." Along the top of a sheet of paper, write a brief description of an upsetting event, particularly one where you behaved in ways you regret. Draw a line to create two columns below the event. In the left column, write down negative or distorted thoughts about the event. In the right column, write down new, alternative thoughts. (Note the mild nature of the word "alternative." The new thoughts are not necessarily highly positive. The goal here is to explore a few possible alternative ways of thinking about the event, and it helps to be gentle with yourself.)

This simple cognitive exercise helps you think more clearly about an emotionally fraught event, identify problematic thought distortions that can be shifted, and empower you to hold yourself accountable for your own wrongdoing in a straightforward way, avoiding the two mistakes of taking too much responsibility for an upsetting event, or too little. Thoughts and feelings can never be completely separated (nor should they be), but to differentiate them in this way can be helpful.

3. Small groups could gather for study and learning about ethical topics, particularly those that challenge them to confront their own participation in harmful systems. The Episcopal Church's *Sacred Ground* curriculum is a good example of a study resource. In a series of videos, readings, and facilitated discussion, groups learn about white supremacy and institutional racism, and they're encouraged to resist the urge to take action before spending time with the material and truly understanding it. (If people rush to do something about a problem, that rush may actually be a form of anxious resistance to the important experience of sitting with the problem—and their part in the problem—so that they can respond or take action later on in a calmer and informed way.) Many of the *Sacred Ground* resources are deeply upsetting for white participants, raising their anxiety and

prompting the other emotions of remorse. But they also offer many opportunities to "think sorry," as participants learn about the structures of injustice and slowly begin to build intercultural competence.

"I CRUCIFIED THEE"

The Good Friday hymn "Ah, Holy Jesus" offers some insight about the intersection of thoughts and feelings in healthy remorse. The text of this hymn is problematic, and for years as a Lutheran church organist, I resisted the recommendation to choose the hymn for services on Good Friday. The text always struck me as gloomy, maudlin, and excessively self-deprecating. I didn't like the underlying theology of atonement either. (And the masculine language in the Episcopal *Hymnal 1982* translation doesn't help.) But I have warmed somewhat to this hymn in recent years—though it is still not one of my favorites—because I now see elements of healthy remorse in it, and specifically "thinking sorry," the cognitive dimension of remorse.

> Ah, holy Jesus, how hast thou offended,
> that man to judge thee hath in hate pretended?
> By foes derided, by thine own rejected,
> O most afflicted!

Who was the guilty? Who brought this upon thee?
Alas, my treason, Jesus, hath undone thee.
'Twas I, Lord Jesus, I it was denied thee;
I crucified thee.

Lo, the Good Shepherd for the sheep is offered;
the slave hath sinned, and the Son hath suffered.
For our atonement, while we nothing heeded,
God interceded.

For me, kind Jesus, was thy incarnation,
thy mortal sorrow, and thy life's oblation;
thy death of anguish and thy bitter passion,
for my salvation.

Therefore, kind Jesus, since I cannot pay thee,
I do adore thee, and will ever pray thee,
think on thy pity and thy love unswerving,
not my deserving.[5]

The first two stanzas ask a series of questions that build
to the blunt statement: "I crucified thee." Even though
the text is strongly emotional, the questions leading up
to that admission of guilt are cognitive questions: this is
about thinking sorry. The singer is working out not only
how the crucifixion makes them feel, but what the crucifixion means. And that meaning is this: the crucifixion is

God's response to human sin, and the appropriate human response to the crucifixion is remorse. Stanzas three and four develop the singer's thoughts, summarizing a complicated theology of atonement in just a few short lines. Finally, in stanza five, the singer prays to God for mercy but, even then, appeals not to any emotions God may have, but to God's cognitive awareness of God's pity and love. This is an old hymn, and it has not aged well in our era. We are more likely to interpret the crucifixion as the triumphant victory over the powers of sin and death or as a liberation from oppression, rather than an act of atonement for sinners (or, as this hymn text is worded, atonement for an individual sinner, each of us driving a nail into the cross). But there is nonetheless a gift for us in this text.

Here is the gift of "Ah Holy Jesus": even when we think about wrongdoing in the form of an old-fashioned hymn, we think about it prayerfully, trusting God's promise of mercy. We are not beating ourselves, or wallowing in shame, using distorted negative thoughts to convict ourselves of dreadful crimes. We are simply owning up to our part in the acts of injustice and evil that have done such terrible damage in the world. When these thoughts and feelings come together in healthy remorse, they turn us toward God's mercy. We are ready to take the next step. We are ready to *say* sorry.

CHAPTER 3

SAYING SORRY

I was probably fourteen years old. I don't remember who was in the hotel room with me that evening, but I am pretty sure it was a bunch of church youth. I can't remember why we were there. We were at the Radisson Hotel in Bloomington, Minnesota, on the I-494 strip. The hotel has a different owner now, so the sign has changed, but you can still whiz by on the freeway and see its hulking shape rising up dully against the sky.

I was a kid from a small town in southwest Minnesota, so a hotel like this seemed glitzy. How extravagant we felt, being in a hotel room and having a party! Everyone was being loud and silly. We were just kids. I think a pillow fight broke out. (It truly is hard to remember the specifics.)

I picked up something heavier than a pillow, maybe a hard plastic cup or some other heavy object, and threw it into the room. The object hit the window and cracked it. I looked at the damaged window and realized that I had essentially vandalized hotel property. I was dizzy with fear.

But I had deniability: because the party was so rowdy, no one saw me throw the object. No one knew which kid did it—except me. Somehow a hotel employee found out about the party and broke it up. And then someone mentioned to him that we had cracked a window. The next thing I remember is being in an office somewhere else in the hotel, along with a couple friends. I do not remember ever fessing up to the crime, though it is possible I did. I do know the hotel employee (probably a manager) knew (1) one of us broke the window; (2) we were scared; and (3) he could mess with us. "If you give us $200," I recall the hotel manager saying, "then we will not call your parents."

This is the moment when I would love to go back in time to advise my younger self. I would knock on the door, and when the manager answered, I would say, "Excuse me, I need to speak to Stephen for a minute. This kid, right here." Then I would take myself out into the hallway and say this: "Stephen, I know you are the one who broke the window. I know because I was there. I saw it happen. Now, please trust me. I know your parents. I know their names and their personal histories." (I would then sketch their histories to prove I knew what I was talking about.) "I know that they will be disappointed and angry, but I also know they will get over this much more quickly than you think. Best of all, I know they will admire you for owning up to what you have done and working to make amends. Let's go and call your parents now, okay? I'll be right there with you when we do."

I, or we kids, figured out how to give the hotel manager $200. (Speaking of wrongdoing, my adult self wonders if he just pocketed the money. Why didn't he just call our parents?) That seemed to be the end of the incident. I returned home and went on with my life, glad to have squeezed out of that jam.

This story is little more than a shard of memory now. I don't have any strong feelings about it. And yet it lingers in my conscious memory all the same. My mother died more than a quarter century ago, and my father would likely find the whole story only mildly interesting. But the pattern I followed that night has recurred a few times over the years.

- I did something wrong, clearly. I made an obviously poor choice.
- I had an opportunity to escape blame and took it.

- I moved forward with my life diminished, retaining a memory of myself as a scofflaw, or at least as an ordinary person who gets into trouble and tries to weasel out of it.

Perhaps this pattern is benign, almost charming, if also a bit pathetic. On the scale of Bad Behaviors in the World, it barely registers. This is not the kind of behavior the Bible talks about. No, the Bible addresses much more grievous sins, such as rapacious greed, sexual violence, murder, genocide. This was just a kid messing around and getting into a tiny crisis, although the same pattern of behavior can be traced in serious crimes. And yet, small though it was, I was truly, deeply scared that night, and it seemed like a dreadful thing to do. And it is still instructive, even now, as a negative example of the power of *saying sorry*.

Saying sorry, the simple act of admitting wrongdoing, allows the wrongdoer to move forward stronger, healthier, and happier, and it opens a door for further work—for making amends (discussed in chapter 4). If I had just admitted what happened and endured the consequences (my parents would have dealt directly with the hotel to settle the bill for the window, and they would have duly punished me for what I did, likely a stern discussion followed by my earning the money to pay them back), I would have a memory of empowerment and self-respect. Even at the age of fourteen, I would have had the integrity to repair what I damaged and then been able to move forward.

My story illustrates how hard it can be to own up to even small infractions and simply say, "I apologize." Imagine how much spiritual sickness people suffer for not apologizing for more serious misbehaviors! They cheat on their spouse; they are fraudulent when reporting business expenses; they lie about something and it costs someone else a job. These offenses will likely require more than a mere apology to repair the damage. But an honest apology is potentially helpful for both the offender and the victim. At the very least, it is a good start.

Apologizing is rarely easy, however. To say "I am sorry" takes courage, even when the offense is minor. To apologize skillfully and effectively often takes practice. And apologies are not always received well. We often look cynically on them—and for good reason. Celebrity offenders hire wordsmiths to craft statements that help them sound contrite without taking responsibility. Legal settlements end with "no admission of wrongdoing." All too often, an offender apologizes to placate or manipulate the person they harmed, which means they are not actually apologizing at all. Saying sorry, then, is complicated. But when it is done honestly and well, it can make remarkable repairs to a broken relationship.

"I APOLOGIZE"

What happens when an apology is not done well? Janis Abrahms Spring is a psychotherapist who specializes in couples therapy, particularly with couples who have been damaged by serious betrayal. In one of her books, *How Can I Forgive You? The Courage to Forgive, the Freedom Not To*, Abrahms Spring reviews a list of poor apologies— apologies that just don't land, that are obviously not authentic. Not only are they worthless, but they often extend the damage done to the hurt party. They include blithe nonapologies such as, "My bad," or conditional apologies such as, "I'm sorry if my comments hurt your feelings," which isn't really an apology at all. Other nonapology apologies are attacks that begin with apology-like words, such as, "I'm sorry you are so sensitive and can't take a joke."

Good apologies are simple, straightforward, and authentic. Saying sorry is often all that is required—when the wrongdoing is not major but significant enough. For example, I recently used the wrong pronoun when mentioning another participant in a meeting. I started to say "she," and even though I didn't get past "sh-" before correcting myself to say "they," I knew they heard it. I knew I messed up. This was an online meeting, so I sent the person a private message and simply said, "Hi, [Name]. I stumbled just now and used the wrong pronoun when referring to you. That was careless, and I apologize." That was it, a two-part apology. First, I stated what I did: carelessly forget their correct pronouns. Second, I simply said, "I apologize." This was not a flip apology, but neither was it overwrought. "I apologize," not "My bad." "I stumbled," not "I'm a piece of crap." And there was not a speck of defensiveness in it. No excuses or groveling. I did not ask them for anything. I did this, and I am sorry.

I knew even as I apologized that I still have a way to go to develop cultural competency with my trans friends and acquaintances, because I have cisgender privilege, and I've been working on this for just a few years. This work includes deepening friendships with trans acquaintances, reading and studying on the topics of gender and sexual identity, and reflecting on my own actions in relationships with others. In that video meeting, I thought about my need to do more of this work. But in the moment I needed to do only one thing: say I was sorry.

AN INTERNET TROLL APOLOGIZES

Saying sorry can be helpful even when someone has inflicted significant harm. Lindy West is a journalist, critic, comedian, and internet personality. She recently produced a situation comedy called *Shrill*, based on her personal memoir of the same name.[1] She concludes this memoir with a story of forgiveness.

Because West's work is typically published on the internet, she often receives unwelcome comments and emails from internet trolls. She accepts these comments as a hazard of her profession. But one particular "troll" cut her more deeply than anyone else. Not long after her father's death, someone created a Twitter account that played on her father's name and from beyond the grave expressed disappointment in his fat daughter. (West writes often about her weight, and on the general topic of the physical appearance of women, from a body-positive perspective.) This person obtained an image of her father and used it as the profile picture for his fraudulent Twitter account. West wrote that she was accustomed to trolling but said, "My armor wasn't strong enough for that."

West knew she should probably ignore him. "Conventional wisdom says, 'Don't engage. It's what they want,'" she writes. "Is it? Are you sure our *silence* isn't what they want? Are you sure they care what we do at all? From where I'm sitting, if I respond, I'm a sucker for taking the bait. If I don't respond, I'm a punching bag."[2]

West decided to write about the experience in a magazine article published one week later. A few hours after her article was posted, she received an email from the troll. To her utter astonishment, he apologized. He explained that his behavior stemmed from self-loathing, yet he did not make excuses. He made a donation to a charity in her father's memory and wished her the best.

West debated how best to respond, but she finally decided to take him at his word and replied to his email. Eventually, they spoke by phone, and their astonishing conversation was broadcast on an episode of the radio show *This American Life*.[3] At one point, West challenges the man by saying, "I mean, have you lost anyone? Can you imagine? Can you imagine?" "I can. I can," he replies. "I don't know what else to say except that I'm sorry." In her memoir, West wrote, "He sounded defeated. I believed him. I didn't mean to forgive him, but I did."[4]

West's conclusion from this unbelievable experience—and it truly beggared belief—was this: "Humans can be reached. I have proof."[5] West is not Christian and contentedly expresses no desire to become one. Yet she articulates here something valuable for Christian communities, something we often fail to consider. "Humans can be reached," West writes, simply. The remorse of this internet troll allowed him to participate in the restoration of his own humanity and to be present to his victim in a way that allowed her to begin recovering from the damage he inflicted upon her.

His remorse motivated one essential action: he apologized, clearly and simply. He did not ask West what he could do to make amends. He did not ask for forgiveness. (She forgave him anyway, almost in spite of herself.) Somehow this person was able to summon something fundamentally decent within himself and offer the person he harmed a simple apology. He said he was sorry. This simple act made a powerful impact on the person he harmed.

APOLOGIZING WITHOUT DEMANDS

Simply saying "I'm sorry" is itself powerful, and in both these stories it might be the best option, at least in the first encounter. However, sometimes we wonder if saying sorry is enough. Perhaps the internet troll could have helped Lindy West more if he had offered to make amends. (He did make a contribution to a charity as a small gesture of apology, but he did not ask her if there was anything more he could do to make amends to her.) When I broke the hotel window, my fourteen-year-old self could have added to my apology, "I want to do what I can to make it right."

That might have been a good thing to say. Or it might have hampered or even prevented the repair I sought.

If I had said, "I'm sorry, I broke the window, and I want to do what I can to make it right," the power of "I'm sorry" could have been diminished. My offer to make amends too quickly could have come across as anxious, suggesting my primary goal was to get out of trouble. I might have truly wanted to fix the problem, and that would not have been wrong. But simply saying "I'm sorry" would have offered the hotel manager and my parents a straightforward acknowledgment of what I did and a chance to tell me what needed to happen next—without my putting pressure on anyone else to do or say anything. I would have simply admitted my guilt.

In the Lindy West story, the internet troll might not have been able to make amends, so an attempt to do so might have done little more than irritate or even further harm her. He seemed instinctively to know there really was nothing he could do to truly repair the damage he inflicted. He could only offer an authentic apology and wish West all the best.

When Christian communities gather Sunday by Sunday and together confess our sins, we do more than apologize. We "say sorry," but then we ask God for forgiveness. Consider this confession of sins in the *Book of Common Prayer:*

Most merciful God,
we confess that we have sinned against you
in thought, word, and deed,
by what we have done,
and by what we have left undone.
We have not loved you with our whole heart;
we have not loved our neighbors as ourselves.
We are truly sorry and we humbly repent.
For the sake of your Son Jesus Christ,
have mercy on us and forgive us;
that we may delight in your will,
and walk in your ways,
to the glory of your Name. Amen.

I wonder if it would be more powerful if we stopped at the line, "We are truly sorry and we humbly repent." This is the concluding line of the first half of the confession, which is purely "saying sorry" and nothing else. When we keep going and ask God for forgiveness, a powerful spiritual experience may be lost—to stand before God and admit guilt, asking God for nothing. This is the power of saying sorry and nothing else: the offender is utterly vulnerable to the victim's response. The victim can simply terminate the relationship, grant forgiveness, or anything in between. The offender asks for nothing.

Consider a corporate apology—from an entire nation to another group of nations—for a particularly atrocious crime. In June 2008, Canadian Prime Minister Stephen Harper published an apology to former students of Indian Residential Schools.[6] Decades of systematic abuse had disrupted countless families and caused the death of thousands of children. Prime Minister Harper's apology is comprehensive, well written, and even compelling. At one point he says "We are sorry," in multiple languages:

> Nous le regrettons
> We are sorry
> Nimitataynan
> Niminchinowesamin
> Mamiattugut

The five languages are French, English, Cree, Anishinaabe, and Inuktitut. This is a poignant apology in large part because the crime was genocidal: children were taken from their families for the express purpose of removing them from their culture and assimilating them into dominant-Canada culture. But even the way these multilingual apologies fall on the page is striking: no punctuation, no prepositional phrases, no adornment of any kind. You can almost hear a solemn bell chiming five times.

Prime Minister Harper did ask for forgiveness just before the five "We are sorry" statements in the five languages. He writes, "The Government of Canada sincerely apologizes and asks the forgiveness of the Aboriginal peoples of this country for failing them so profoundly." But it is almost said in passing and could be taken out of the sentence without robbing it—or the letter—of its power. It follows an exhaustive recounting of the many crimes for which the Canadian government is profoundly sorry, and the whole letter overall is a near-perfect example of "saying sorry" and doing nothing else. And how could the government do otherwise? They can't go back and save the thousands of children who were killed. They can't restore the families whose children were forcibly removed. They can't undo decades of genocidal violence and forced assimilation. But as the letter says in its conclusion, they can establish a truth and reconciliation commission (similar to the one established in South Africa after the fall of apartheid) designed to "educate all Canadians on the Indian Residential Schools system"—or as I would call it, *thinking sorry.* It may take another century to move beyond apology to the work of relationship repair, the work of forgiveness, but the work has begun.

Small mistakes often require a basic apology: "I'm sorry." But larger ones, as we have seen, can also call for "I/we are sorry," and nothing more. Whether you're a silly kid who breaks a hotel window, an internet troll who attacks a journalist, or a whole nation owning up to a century of genocidal violence, saying sorry, and only saying sorry, may be what's called for.

AFTER SAYING SORRY

Even when saying sorry is enough, we have another task: to receive the response of the person we have apologized to. They might respond without words but with a nod, a smile, a scowl or frown, a shrug. They might respond with tears—of joy or relief or anger. They might reach out for a hug. They might tell us what they are thinking or how they are feeling in the moment. They might reveal how the harm has affected them since it occurred. They might respond immediately or not for many months—if ever. Whatever their response, we complete the communication circle by receiving it.

Sometime in the first year of my sobriety, I talked with one of my sisters about my recovery. This sister and I had been close companions in our early childhoods and again when we were teenagers. As we became adults, we were not as close but still always friendly. She told me she felt deep relief when she heard that I had gotten sober, something several people told me in those early months. I did not always react well when someone said this. When a workplace friend said it, I became angry with her and indulged my insecurity, accusing her of patronizing me. (We soon reconciled.) But this time, when my sister said it, I did not feel defensive. I just felt sorry.

I felt sorry when my sister said she was relieved about my sobriety because she also said this: "Honestly, you scared me with your drinking. You seemed dangerous to me. I was intimidated, and I worried about you." I am grateful now that when she said this, I did not anxiously or angrily mount a defense. I felt empathy for the fear she had felt, and I regretted doing things that frightened her.

I apologized, and that is all that I did. I did not say, "I want to do anything I can to make things right." It wouldn't necessarily have been wrong or harmful to say that, but my simple, clean apology felt right. It was true. If I had gone ahead and said, "I want to do anything I can to make things right," I could have placed a burden on her to tell me what I needed to do, to focus on me, to melodramatically make the conversation all about me. I could have obscured the truth that other than staying sober and trying not to do more damage, there wasn't any restoration to make, no practical repairs to my sister's possessions or finances, nothing really to do or to say beyond, "I'm sorry." I had scared her. In sobriety I felt bad about that, and apologized. Saying sorry was enough. Hearing her words of concern closed the circle.

GOOD FRIDAY

In the Episcopal Church, the liturgy for Good Friday opens with this prayer:

> Almighty God, we pray you graciously to behold this your family, for whom our Lord Jesus Christ was willing to be betrayed, and given into the hands of sinners, and to suffer death upon the cross; who now lives and reigns with you and the Holy Spirit, one God, for ever and ever. Amen.

Notice how the faithful only ask God for one thing: *to look at us.* This Good Friday collect doesn't say the specific words, "We are sorry," but the intent is similar. We stand before God, well aware of our brokenness and culpability. And we ask God only to look at us. Amends may come in due time, and Christian life as a whole can be understood as making amends. With God's help, we repair our relationships with each other, with our neighbor, with the whole planet. But there is great power in this moment of truth, as we stand in God's presence. There is great power in simply saying, whether to another person or to God, "We are sorry."

CHAPTER 4

DOING SORRY

Andrew and I had to rebuild our marriage. The alcohol bottle had been at the center of our marriage for years, and even though I was the physical alcoholic—and I alone was responsible for all my mistakes and poor choices—we did not know how to be married without my drinking problem.

In the early weeks of sobriety, I didn't know what to do on Friday evenings. By early 2013, I was suffering from moderate to severe alcohol dependence, so I drank every day at many times of the day, but Friday-evening cocktails were a particular moment of connection in our marriage, an opportunity to have a cocktail and settle in for a quiet evening. The cocktails felt like a lubricant for conversation and connection, although I never connected deeply with anyone in those days, and often by late Friday evening I was out cold, only to awaken in the wee hours feeling sick, fearful of what I might have said the evening before while in a blackout.

"What am I supposed to do?" I texted my AA sponsor on one of those first Friday evenings. He offered bracing advice. "Just get up, go downstairs, and talk to your husband. You can drink water, it tastes fine, and in any case it's not about what you're drinking. It's about you and your husband." My sponsor told me that he now goes with friends on wine tours and drinks water while they taste the wines. "Sometimes I ask the winery staff about their craft and how they run their business," he said. "But mostly I talk with my friends, catch up with them, have a good time with them. I don't need to drink the wine. And they don't need to either, but they enjoy it and know how to enjoy it well, so I hang out with them while they pursue that interest, and we all have a good time."

As the weeks passed, I let my sponsor's good-natured enthusiasm guide me in my efforts to rebuild my marriage. I found going with Andrew to a winery unthinkable, but I also felt guilty about that: we had often gone to wineries and even designed long weekends around winery tours. He would taste the wine; I would drink to get drunk. Only very recently, nine years into my sobriety, we entered a winery tasting room so he could pick up a shipment of bottles. (It will take him and our friends several weeks to move through those bottles; in my drinking days, the supply dwindled fast.) Being in a winery again—smelling the lovely, yeasty aroma of the wine, admiring the gleaming granite countertops and the rows of sparkling glasses—felt odd. We didn't linger; Andrew picked up his shipment and we left for lunch. Maybe in year ten, or twelve, I'll go with him and talk to him while he tastes a few of their wines.

By August 2013, three months into sobriety, I felt restless. I had many more hours in the day. I was sleeping better, eating better, feeling better, and wanting to start making changes. We had an uncomfortable conversation one afternoon. I was now capable of connection and was eager to draw closer in conversation, to explore and evaluate our relationship. Andrew had his own process, his own experience, during this time. We struggled to connect. I felt frustrated and impatient.

Sometime into the first year of sobriety, we attended a weekend retreat for couples in recovery. We learned together what I had been told in outpatient rehab: when someone gets sober, their spouse and family go through a parallel recovery process. I had learned that blood tests of newly sober addicts and their family members have many of the same markers of addiction, which suggests that even if there is only one physical user in the family, everyone bears physical symptoms of addiction, alongside all the emotional and relational problems.

This retreat was good for us. It gave us time to be together and to focus on our marriage. I admit we felt some relief that we were not the unhappiest couple in the room. But it was worrying when one couple erupted in conflict, derailing the whole class for a while. In my marriage, we don't erupt much. Both of us prefer to close a conflict as soon as we can, and a deeper joy of our marriage is that our core friendship has been intact throughout. Even in the worst days of my alcoholism, our friendship survived.

But that friendship didn't thrive in the first years of my sobriety. Both of us were busy learning how to respond to all my changes. As I mentioned in chapter 2, I began working with a new sponsor and focused with him on the damage I had done to my marriage and other friendships. But that new sponsor relationship didn't really take off. I realized in working Step 5 that I was not yet ready to address some of the problems.

Slowly and fitfully, I began making amends to my husband for the damage I had done to our marriage, our friendship, and Andrew himself. But the amends weren't going to be a simple matter of apologizing and making restitution, the way a recovering alcoholic might apologize to someone they defrauded and repay them the amount they stole. I needed to work out a new ethic, a new way of being a husband. I needed to enact in my daily life the values I claimed in AA meetings and in my own self-understanding. I needed to grow up. I needed to build a new life and work with my husband to build a new marriage in the center of that life. I needed to *do sorry*.

REBUILDING

A story from Genesis offers wisdom on "doing sorry." In Genesis 11, God sees that the people are building a new tower—probably a ziggurat, a common building set aside for sacred rituals in ancient Mesopotamia. God knows the monoculture that gave rise to this tower is potentially dangerous: "Look, they are one people, and they all have one language, and this is only the beginning of what they will do; nothing that they propose to do will now be impossible for them" (Genesis 11:6). The Tower of Babel is frequently interpreted as a story of hubris: the people's sin was that they wanted to be as powerful as God. But the story may help us understand "doing sorry" more deeply, too. It can help us see how human wrongdoing leads to a shattering of what was and offers an opportunity to rebuild something new.

Consider this interpretation of the Genesis 11 story: God is concerned about the people because they are limited in their imagination. They are making no room for diversity, new ideas, or constructive conflict. They have no healthy or loyal opposition. They are a monoculture descending into hubris, patterns of misbehavior, sinful actions—and away from God. Ironically, their effort to construct a large tower makes them *smaller*, the way my substance abuse made me a smaller person in so many ways—limited in my imagination, an unfaithful friend, a disappointing spouse. So God "confuses their language," making it impossible for them to communicate, and they abandon the tower project and scatter in all directions. No longer one group of people working closely with coordination, they are now helter-skelter, lost in chaos, and their ambitions and abilities have gotten much smaller. If they want to recover, they will have to rebuild.

When I first got sober, the life I had led in my drinking days was shattered. In the immediate wake of my arrest, I felt like my life was in pieces, and I had all kinds of rebuilding to do. I began feeling, thinking, and saying sorry, but I also had to rebuild my life—my marriage, my finances, my friendships, my career, my physical health.

All of this was necessary because I had been in the wrong. Like those ancient tower builders, I was misbehaving. And I was guilty of deceit: I tried to hide my drinking from my husband and others. I pretended to clients and friends alike that all was well. When I was an active alcoholic, I often behaved in ways that pressured friends and family members to be the more mature and responsible person. My childish behavior drew other adults into an inappropriate parent–child dynamic. (For example, my husband had to work with one of my siblings to get me home safely one evening when I was passed out in the passenger seat of the car.)

As I began to recover, I couldn't just feel sorry, think sorry, and say sorry: I needed to do sorry. I needed to rebuild my life by developing behavior patterns with others that built trust, showing up on time every time, readily admitting mistakes and making repairs. Often—it's accurate to say nearly constantly—in AA culture, one is reminded that only a higher power can truly bring about recovery. For me, that higher power begins this work by shattering my old behaviors, assumptions, and even self-understanding— by "confusing the language" of my drinking self. Once my old self has been shattered, my higher power can re-create me as a new and healthier person, one rebuilt relationship at a time.

REBUILDING AFTER THE AFFAIR

An individual's recovery from substance abuse offers a vivid example of "shattering and rebuilding"—the need for and the process of "doing sorry." But other examples help us understand this aspect of remorse.

Extramarital affairs are shattering experiences that can (or at least should) lead a remorseful person to rebuild their life and relationships. In my work as a couples psychotherapist, the revelation of an affair usually accompanied the revelation of other behaviors—often committed by both people in the relationship—that led the couple to a crisis point. Nevertheless, it was typically helpful to identify one member of the couple as the "offender," at least in the beginning stages of repairing the relationship.

An affair can shatter nearly everything the other person had assumed to be true about the marriage and the person they married. Sometimes even the person who had the affair is shocked by their own behavior. The therapist's job is to join with both persons in an authentic therapeutic bond. To make these connections, it's a good idea—arguably a necessity—for the therapist to meet one-on-one with each member of the couple in the assessment stage, so both people will feel safe and motivated to engage in treatment.

For the therapist to connect with the person who did not have the affair is often uncomplicated. They need the therapist to understand fully how they feel and what they think. They need the therapist's allegiance and commitment to help them make their way through the problem. They need a skillful and friendly clinician. But the therapist must also connect with the offender, usually someone who does not want to accept the title of "offender" and is understandably apprehensive about being judged or rejected by the therapist. When I worked with couples grappling with this problem, I could usually tell from the offender's behavior and our interaction in the initial one-on-one appointment how well the overall course of therapy would go. If I as a therapist could not empathize with the offender, then I would likely not help the couple at all. But if the offender could not face what they did and empathize with their partner's trauma, then that was also a worrying sign that therapy would be difficult.

I approached these conversations mindful of my own history of betrayal and wrongdoing. I have lied to my husband. I have misled co-workers. I have let down clients and supervisors alike. I once stole a tiny Big Bird toy from a childhood friend. I wouldn't necessarily tell these stories to my clients, but when I was in the room with a client who had betrayed their partner, I could readily acknowledge that I am fallible, that I have done wrong, and that I am still capable of behaving ethically. Though I have lied to my husband, I am not fundamentally a bad husband. Though I have behaved badly in the workplace, I am not fundamentally a bad coworker or employee. Though I stole from my childhood friend, I can be a trustworthy friend today—in large part because I readily admit that I once stole from a friend! In other words, I have done, and still do, the work of remorse. Sometimes the remorse is little more than saying to myself, "Whoops, that was a mistake," and going forward with a renewed determination to do better. Other times, I admit that I hurt someone and need to make a repair. In all these cases, when I simply feel, think, say, and finally *do* "sorry," I not only feel better, but I am a better husband, colleague, and friend. And so, as I talk with the offender in a couple grappling with a major betrayal, I offer them genuine empathy and can join therapeutically with them. I can even ask bracing questions like, "So, can you admit that what you did was hurtful?"

If the offender can admit wrongdoing, then they are ready to begin rebuilding their marriage. They are ready to apologize authentically, and sometimes at some length, with no conditions and no "but you hurt me, too" comments. They can also begin to earn the other person's forgiveness by building new daily patterns of reliably trustworthy behaviors. Many couples in the first stages of the repair need to accommodate the hurt person's hypervigilant behaviors. The hurt person may want to check the offender's phone, or ask where they've been all day, or receive repeated apologies. They may need the offender to listen attentively and remain nondefensive while they recount how they felt when they discovered the affair. Responding nondefensively on so many fronts is hard for the offender to do! But it does lead to a rebuilding of trust. Shattered by the betrayal, the couple slowly draws closer together again and rebuilds a new relationship.

Meanwhile, the offender can get in touch with their deeper feelings and struggles, which can be healing for them, too. In my work as a couples therapist, I would sometimes do what John and Julie Gottman call the "Dan Wile Technique," named after a clinician who designed this particular intervention.[1] I would say to the offender, "If you like, I could speak to your spouse as if I were you. I will tell them how you feel, and what you think. I will even move my chair, so I am in a spot different from my usual 'therapist' place and stance. When I'm done, I'll check with you to be sure that what I said in your voice, on your behalf, was accurate. You'll have a chance to correct me." The clients always gave me permission to do this.

(I believe they might be curious about what I might say, in addition to needing help expressing their own feelings.) Here is an approximate quote of what I might say, speaking as if I were the offender in a couple grappling with a major betrayal. (In a session with an actual couple, I would include many more details grounded in my assessment of the couple, and of the offender in particular.)

Susan, I am in the wrong. I know that. I should not have hurt you, and there is no excuse. I have apologized, and will keep apologizing, with sincerity. But I want to say something more about what was going on for me when I did this. Please know I say all this not as an excuse, but because I want you to know a deeper truth about me. Nothing excuses my behavior. I know that. But I want you to know how sad and lonely I have felt, for a long time. I have had hurt feelings, and I haven't handled those well. It's hard for me to admit to myself that I feel hurt, that I am sad, that I want to be closer to you. It's also hard for me to acknowledge that you feel this way too, because I know I have pushed you away. It was easier to act out or do something that puts the feelings off for a while. It was easier to behave in ways that are hurtful. But by doing all this, I broke my own rules about how to be a good spouse. I hurt you, and that's what's most important. But I betrayed my own best self, too. I am trying to own my hurtful behaviors. I am working hard to walk the walk as a grown adult who knows right from wrong. I have missed you, and I have felt so lonely and sad. I want you to know how much I love you, and long for you, and hope that I can make a real repair with you.

This is the work of remorse, the labor of doing sorry. It offers profound benefits for offenders and victims alike. Every time I used the Dan Wile technique, I guessed that the offender felt deep sadness beneath their defensiveness and resentment—and every time I was correct. This wasn't because I possessed uncommon wisdom about how people feel and think. The couples therapist Sue Johnson, who uses psychological attachment theory in her work with couples, demonstrates consistently that hurtful behaviors always arise in the context of the offender's own hurt feelings.[2] When these deeper, more tender feelings are surfaced and expressed, both people feel better, and they begin the work of rebuilding their bond.

If the healing proceeds and trust grows, the hurt person can eventually talk about their part in a toxic relational pattern that may have been up and running in the weeks, months, and years that preceded the affair. This is not the same as accepting blame for the affair itself: the offender remains authentically remorseful and fully owns their culpability for their spouse's pain. But the new, rebuilt relationship eventually makes room for both people to do the healthy work of remorse in response to anything they had done to damage their bond.

SIBLINGS REBUILD A FRIENDSHIP

A few years ago, I was involved in an intense conflict with one of my sisters. She didn't want to speak to me for several months, and it was more than a year before we found our way back to a friendly, yet initially distant, relationship.

The conflict story began on a late December afternoon, when I was at a Seattle Seahawks game with a friend. My sister texted me and said she wanted to call. I knew this was a call I needed to take, the way you know about such things. I left my seat in the stadium and found a relatively quiet corner in an outer corridor of the complex. My sister told me that our uncle, our father's brother, had died that day. She added that he had left a substantial estate to all of us, his seven nieces and nephews.

The only previous time our family had suffered bitter conflict was in 1996, when my mother died. I didn't anticipate that this would happen again, but it did, though in different ways, along different fault lines. We didn't squabble about my uncle's estate: I am happy to report that not one of us behaved badly or even insensitively about the inheritance issues. But tensions did arise, in part because we didn't all work equally in caring for our uncle when he endured his last, long illness. I lived in Seattle the whole time, while others—particularly the sister with whom I had conflict—remained in Minnesota and paid him many more visits, sometimes involving complicated hospital trips and other chores. There were other seeds of conflict. In large families with powerful personalities, resentments can emerge quickly, for lots of reasons. Relationships between any two people are complicated, but these complications are deepened by the intricate web of relationships across the family.

After many months, turning into years, of administering my uncle's estate, we were approaching the end: the final sale of his house and the final disbursements of funds from the account that my sister was managing. By this time, my conflict with my sister was significant, and it was complicated by misunderstandings, indirect communication, and the strain and stress of our respective home and work lives.

Finally, on a winter morning (I remember exactly where I was when it happened, because it was so upsetting), we had a rough email exchange. I felt dismissed and misunderstood, but I did not behave as well as I should have. Unfortunately, we did not have in place a reliable process of repair in which we could express remorse for ordinary misbehavior. (This is why I wrote this book!) And so my sister and I lost more than a year of friendship, all because we couldn't, or chose not to, reconcile.

I flew to Minnesota for a visit several years later and saw my sister for the first time since our hard conflict. We met at a diner near her house. My sister was bright, lively, sensitive, and friendly throughout the conversation. I was working with a therapist back in Virginia at the time, near where I was attending seminary, and the therapist had predicted that the reconciliation would look something like this: we would find our way to a cautious peace, but we would likely not really talk through everything (and we might not need to). At this point in the story, my therapist was right. As our breakfast at the diner drew to an end, my sister looked at me and said, simply, "I love you." Tears sprung at the edges of her eyes. "I love you too," I replied. I meant it. And that truly was all we said about the conflict, at the time.

Through all of this, in the months before and after this encounter at the diner, I tried to practice amends with my other siblings and in my other friendships. I deliberately (and successfully!) stepped out of the usual triangulations and other communication patterns in the family, patterns that had fed many of our conflicts. I replied to messages in quietly friendly ways. I remember through all those months feeling more distant from everyone in my family except perhaps my father, but I also felt better, because I was not doing what I had done that had harmed my sister. I did not want to repeat the conflict in other places, with other people, and I was able to honor that promise to myself.

Then, two years later, in a conversation with my sister during another visit to Minnesota, she unexpectedly brought up the conflict and mentioned our cautious rapprochement in the diner. We were in her backyard, playing with her dogs. My sister said, "I want to apologize to you. I am sorry. In this family, we sometimes think things about each other that aren't accurate and aren't kind, and I don't want to do that anymore. I really am sorry." I was shocked and moved. I didn't know what to say. But over the hours, and then the days, that followed that conversation, I felt a deeper sense of joy and contentment, and love, not only for my sister, but for my whole family. I felt a new sense of hope in our family's future.

Much of the credit for that repair goes to my sister. She made partial amends with me, and we later made a complete repair. But I also feel satisfied and grateful for the amends I was able to make in this conflict. I was able to avoid damaging others in ways similar to the damage

I did to my sister. And I was able to do that simply by doing basic remorse work: assessing my own behavior in the clear light of day, with both cognitive and affective self-awareness, and acting differently. I believe I slowly became the kind of brother that one can approach to make a good repair. I feel deep joy about this.

THE EPISCOPAL CHURCH RECKONS WITH ALCOHOLISM

"Doing sorry," like all the other dimensions of remorse (feeling, thinking, and saying sorry) is done by individuals, couples, and families. But it is also done by larger groups, and sometimes whole churches and even church denominations. The Episcopal Church did important remorse work following a terrible tragedy caused by an Episcopal bishop.

In late December 2014, two days after Christmas, a car struck and killed Thomas Palermo, a Baltimore software engineer who worked at Johns Hopkins Hospital. Palermo was the father of two young children, six and four years old. He was known and loved by many in the Baltimore cycling community and is remembered as an enthusiastic bicyclist. "'Tom was a magical character,'" said a friend. "'He had a glint in his eye. He was such a sweetheart and had such a lovely family.'"[3] As the Palermo family and their friends reeled from this news, the local media learned that the driver of the SUV that struck him was the Rt. Rev. Heather Cook, one of the Episcopal bishops in the diocese of Maryland. Her role drew national attention to the story and led to efforts in the Episcopal Church to confront broadly the problem of substance abuse.

The Episcopal Church, in General Convention in July 2015, concurred on three separate resolutions that addressed the problem of substance abuse: a policy that addresses the misuse and abuse of alcohol at church events and on church properties, a resolution supporting "healing ministries to those affected by addiction," and a resolution addressing how aspirants for Holy Orders may be evaluated for possible substance abuse.[4] I served on the committee that supervised this legislation. In our daily gatherings during the convention, the committee began each session with prayer and provided time for each deputy to share their personal histories and perspectives on the issue. The Baltimore drunk-driving incident had occurred just half a year before. It was a topic of many conversations as the committee went about its work. The committee sensed that something tangible and significant must be done; the church must respond; the church must change. That the whole convention of bishops and deputies approved the resolutions demonstrated a willingness, if not determination, to "do sorry."

While it's commendable that the Episcopal Church passed these resolutions, it remains to be seen whether deep and lasting change will happen. Communal remorse can be hard to do, hard to sustain. Dioceses and congregations may comply with the new resolutions by changing how and whether they include alcohol in their gatherings and taking seriously the need to address substance-abuse problems in their discernment with those in formation as deacons, priests, and bishops. But I worry that the easy comfort many Episcopalians feel with the problematic presence of alcohol in church culture will largely remain in place. I am concerned that the wake-up call of Bishop Cook's incident has already receded in our shared memory, and a deeper reckoning with alcohol in our culture may not be done.

The sincere concern of many in the wake of Heather Cook's incident[5] should not be doubted. Episcopalians gather in General Convention with serious purpose. We also gratefully acknowledge that God hears our prayers of remorse, however halting or infrequent, in their full sincerity. Many Episcopalians authentically wonder: were we all, in some way, responsible? But I remain concerned that it will be all too easy to settle back into old patterns that led to the tragedy in Baltimore. In the weeks following the incident, reporters discovered that members of Bishop Cook's diocese had expressed concerns to other bishops about her drinking, and nothing had been done about the problem. Many leaders in the church spoke more broadly about the problematic role alcohol plays in many Episcopal gatherings. (Jokes about Episcopalians often poke fun at the abundant presence of alcohol in Episcopal meetings and celebrations.) Will the 2014 tragedy prove to be a turning point for the Episcopal Church on this issue?

One vignette from the 2015 Convention deliberations is telling. The committee on substance abuse prepared much of the written content of the resolutions, including the resolution recommending language for policies to be adopted at the parish level addressing alcohol use in parish life. For example, many churches offer formation events with images of alcohol in the title, such as "Theology on Tap" or "Wine and Cheese Night." The committee included a plank about these titles, recommending modestly that congregations try to resist the urge to use them. In an off-the-record conversation, one deputy speculated that including such a plank might prove to be good political strategy: it likely would be removed by amendment, giving the larger deliberative body a satisfying sense that they are offering healthy critique of the language while leaving the bulk of the resolution intact. That, in fact, happened. The "Theology on Tap" language was quickly deleted, and the resolution passed handily.

These are expectable, even ordinary political machinations inherent to any polity gathering in convention. One could even argue that alcohol-themed titles of various parish ministries are relatively harmless. But the quick dismissal of the plank is worrisome. Why do Episcopalians so enjoy these references to alcohol? Perhaps they make us appear "hip," "with it." "Theology on Tap" communicates friendliness, openness, tolerance. These titles are not inherently unethical, let alone evil. Those who adopt these titles usually have good intentions, and most people should be given the benefit of the doubt. And yet the endurance of these cultural artifacts leads me to doubt the sincerity of our statements of deep concern about the terrible events of that day, and more broadly about the use of alcohol in Episcopal gatherings, and in the cultures of our churches and dioceses.

Now, the 2015 resolutions weren't a total failure. They are still on the books in the Episcopal Church. Many dioceses and congregations are doubtlessly more conscious now about substance-abuse problems in their congregational cultures. Nevertheless, the Episcopal Church can do more, and do better. We can *do sorry*. In preaching, teaching, and pastoral care, faith leaders (both lay and clergy) can name the presence and power of substance abuse in individual and family life. They can:

- talk openly about it
- invite other people to speak openly about it
- stay informed about the science of addiction and recovery
- study Scripture as a way to reflect on substance abuse and communal recovery
- be an ally and friend to those who are struggling with substance abuse
- support advocacy ministries in their local contexts on behalf of communities damaged by substance abuse

In all these actions, the Episcopal Church as a whole can *do sorry* for the damage inflicted not just on the Palermo family, but on all victims of substance abuse and addiction. We cannot return Tom Palermo from the dead, but our work of amends, driven by healthy remorse, is one way to participate in the resurrection of Christ that continues to re-create the world.

RESTORING THE DIGNITY OF HUMAN NATURE

This is the appointed collect in the Episcopal *Book of Common Prayer* for the Second Sunday after Christmas:[6]

> O God, who wonderfully created, and yet more wonderfully restored, the dignity of human nature: Grant that we may share the divine life of him who humbled himself to share our humanity, your Son Jesus Christ; who lives and reigns with you, in the unity of the Holy Spirit, one God, for ever and ever. Amen.

This collect shares a bit of language from the Roman eucharistic rite, which includes a prayer spoken by the deacon as they set the Eucharistic Table. As the deacon pours a little water into the wine, they say this prayer: "By the mystery of this water and wine, may we share in your divinity, as you humbled yourself to share in our humanity." Both prayers—the Christmastide collect and the Catholic Table prayer—celebrate the incarnation of Jesus Christ as an event that transforms the human race, allowing us to share in God's divine life. But the collect says more: the incarnation restores the dignity of humans "yet more wonderfully" than it was when that dignity was created in the first place! The redemptive work of Christ is an act of re-creation that exceeds the wonder of the original creation.

Note also that the collect focuses on human dignity as something created, and then restored, by God. God did not just create humanity; God created our dignity. Dignity is an English word descended from the Latin word *dignus,* which means "worthy." Our worth, our value, our identity as beings who matter: God created this, and God restores this. When we do the work of remorse—when we *do sorry*—we are participating in God's restoration of our worth, our dignity. The title "offender" takes up its quotation marks again, and then is discarded altogether: the offender is once again something more, something better. Their dignity has been restored. Indeed, it has been restored to something better than it had been before the wrongdoing.

This, then, is the great gift of doing sorry: it makes us better than we were before we committed the sin that led to our healthy remorse. The recovering alcoholic becomes a better husband, friend, and coworker than he was before he started drinking problematically. The spouse who had an affair and works to rebuild their marriage becomes a better spouse than they were before the affair happened. The rebuilt marriage is better than the happy union the couple celebrated on their wedding day. The brother and sister are closer friends than they were before their up-setting conflict. The congregation that handles alcohol responsibly in the wake of a serious reckoning becomes more mature and safer than they were before. Doing sorry doesn't just fix what's broken: it improves on the original design.

This improvement leads to deep joy, and it is that joy to which we now turn.

CHAPTER 5

THAT YOUR JOY MAY BE COMPLETE

_____

Jesus said to them, "I have said these things to you so that my joy may be in you, and that your joy may be complete."

—JOHN 15:11

On May 24, 2014, I got in the car to drive to Tukwila, a suburb of Seattle where the facility that services breathalyzers installed in private automobiles is located. This had been my routine every month since I first sobered up. They would check the system for any violations and reset my device, and their written report was evidence that I remained in compliance and had not even once failed a breathalyzer test. But this time, I was driving there to have the device *removed.* I had completed the one-year requirement. This part of my probation was done. I believe I still had monthly check-in appointments at the outpatient re-hab clinic, but even those were low key, just routine things on my to-do list. (I honestly can't remember exactly when that obligation was also completed: it is all so long ago now. My sobriety has been stable ever since.) I sensed on May 24, 2014, however, that this was an important day. The breathalyzer was a burden not only for me, but for my husband. It was a strong irritant in our daily routine: you had to blow into it whenever it sounded its alarm, not just when first starting the car. It followed a random pat-tern, so the device would beep at lots of different times, including the few seconds after you parked and before you turned off the car to, say, go into a meeting that you al-ready were running late to attend. Removing this device was a triumph.

After the device was gone, I joyfully drove back to Seattle and treated myself, or really the car, to a deluxe car wash at the iconic Elephant Car Wash on Denny Way. I filled the tank with gas, and drove home, where the car proudly stood until Andrew could come home and see that we had gotten our freedom back.

In those days, one of the AA meetings I attended recited the AA "Promises" at each meeting. The Promises speak of the deep joy and contentment that awaits the recover-ing alcoholic who works the program. I experienced these

Promises on that joyful spring day when the breathalyzer was removed. But these Promises are also—for me—a description of the deep joy that follows healthy remorse:

If we are painstaking about this phase of our development, we will be amazed before we are half way through. We are going to know a new freedom and a new happiness. We will not regret the past nor wish to shut the door on it. We will comprehend the word serenity and we will know peace. No matter how far down the scale we have gone, we will see how our experience can benefit others. That feeling of uselessness and self-pity will disappear. We will lose interest in selfish things and gain interest in our fellows. Self-seeking will slip away. Our whole attitude and outlook upon life will change. Fear of people and of economic insecurity will leave us. We will intuitively know how to handle situations which used to baffle us. We will suddenly realize that God is doing for us what we could not do for ourselves. Are these extravagant promises? We think not. They are being fulfilled among us—sometimes quickly, sometimes slowly. They will always materialize if we work for them.[1]

Sometimes when the Promises are recited at an AA meeting, everyone chants "Work, work, work!" as the reader finishes the last phrase, "if we work for them." Another popular AA saying is, "It works if you work it." I once again speak only for myself, but this "work" is more than just recovering from substance abuse. It is the work of healthy remorse: recognizing that I have done something I shouldn't have, feeling the hard feelings of guilt and regret, thinking through what happened and how I am responsible, apologizing to the person(s) I harmed, and rebuilding whatever I shattered through my bad behavior. This work leads to joy. Remorse is a path into bright gladness. I feel deep and profound relief, but I also feel stronger—stronger than I was before I did my remorse work, and stronger than I was even before I misbehaved in the first place. I believe deep joy awaits those who do the work—always with God's help—of healthy remorse.

RUNNING A HALF MARATHON

In December 2014, I signed up to run a half marathon, 13.1 miles. The race was scheduled for March 22, 2015, and the course takes runners around Mercer Island, east of Seattle. I was nervous as I pressed "enter" on the online order form. It seemed close to impossible that I could actually do this.

In January 2015, I started suffering sharp right-knee pain on my training runs. For the first time in my life, I began a course of acupuncture alongside physical therapy. Slowly I regained the ability to run without pain. I still remember one of my first shorter runs after a few weeks of walking and therapy. I ran about a mile along the paved trail in Myrtle Edwards Park, near the water on the north shore of Elliott Bay. I pushed it a little too far that day, but I recovered. I made it to race day.

As I turned west along the shore of Mercer Island, about halfway through the half marathon, I started feeling serious pain in my left foot. I was determined not to stop, not even to slow down. In a flash of inspiration, I prayed. "Dear Jesus," I prayed (in a style much simpler and more earnest than my usual prayer practice), "help my foot feel a little stronger." I don't typically think God answers prayers in such direct ways, but my foot did feel stronger. I finished the race.

As I began trudging up the long hill between mile posts 11 and 12, someone started running alongside me. I clearly remember him seeming to be in far better shape than me, if not physically (I was in decent physical shape), then certainly in his ability to run at that particular point. He didn't tell me his name. He made light conversation with me and said gently encouraging things. At some point between mile posts 12 and 13, he either ran ahead or dropped behind. He was gone. Later, after the race was done, I wondered if he was a volunteer with the organization hosting the race, jumping into the run to encourage people as they finished the hardest mile. He was no angel:

I am not going to say he was God's messenger, human or otherwise. He was simply a good person who was helping out that day—officially or not, I cannot say. He was there for me.

This is yet another story of joy in the wake of healthy remorse. My sobriety story is not simply a story of healing or substance-abuse recovery. It is not only a story of my higher power doing for me what I cannot do for myself. It *is* those things. But it is more: it is a story of healthy remorse.

When I was drinking, I was silly. I was sloppy. I was a little fraudulent. I say a "little" fraudulent because I did not embezzle; I did not sleep around on my husband; I did not force someone else to take the blame for my crimes. The only crime I committed was driving while intoxicated. Now, that is not a "little" crime! It is serious, dead serious. But it is not in the "fraud" column as much as it might be in the "careless" column. It is the behavior of someone who is living heedlessly, living dangerously, living selfishly and destructively.

I was not corrupt as much as I was ridiculous. I was not deceitful as much as I was pathetic. When I drank excessively, I got progressively sillier and more raucous, and then I would black out, stop drinking, slow down, and collapse. There were a couple of domestic scenes in which I was not abusive, but I was nonetheless not at all fun to have around. In the years before my alcoholism progressed from moderate to low-severe, I would sometimes throw up—in the bed, in the car—and this would be a source of deep shame for me and understandable anger for my husband. But I did not ever strike him or betray him in ways that were truly shocking, let alone cruel. I was just a sad mess.

All of this meant that my task in sobriety was to "go and sin no more," as Jesus memorably says. My entire story of sobriety is a story of living amends, dotted by occasional acts of direct amends. I readily admit, though, that some of the amends I need to make are connected to *post-sobriety* behaviors! (Note that in all the examples of conflict with my siblings, my misbehavior occurred after I got sober!) The remorse work that I do—the remorse that I try to practice—includes working Step 10 in Alcoholics Anonymous: "We continued to take personal inventory, and when we were wrong, fully admitted it." When I do this work, I not only stay sober: I feel better. Even joyful.

THE SORROW AND JOY OF GOD'S EASTER PEOPLE

Through all these years of substance abuse and sobriety, misbehavior and making amends, anguish and deep relief,

I have worked as a deacon and priest in Episcopal congregations in Washington state and Virginia. I have gathered during the week with AA friends, and then worked with the "upstairs people" who gather on Sundays for worship. And while the AA Promises are written and meant for people in recovery from substance abuse, the joys of healthy remorse await all people, provided we do the work.

Certain liturgical practices may help penitent Christians express and work on remorse and experience the great joy that follows. Eastertide is the most festive season of the liturgical year, but ironically it may be the best season to do the work of remorse. The readings and prayers of Easter recall how the first witnesses to the resurrection experienced both sorrow and joy, terror and relief. They were shaken not only by their contemplation of God's mighty acts, but also by their own participation in the handing over of Jesus to judgment and death. And so for us, the Easter season is abundantly joyful, but it is not just a festive party. On that first Easter and ever since, the resurrected Christ appears to people who have done the wrong thing, breathes peace upon them, and invites them into new life that is better than anything they experienced before.

Episcopal priest Marion Hatchett, a contributor to the *Book of Common Prayer*, briefly reviews in his *Commentary on the American Prayer Book* the Reformation-era history of the rite of confession. Hatchett's description of the rite, and particularly his explanation of the rubric that allows for its omission on festal days, raises an intriguing question. He notes that a "confession of sin on the part of the whole congregation was new to the liturgies of the Reformation period," because "in the early church Christians acknowledged their sinfulness by giving thanks to God, in the eucharistic prayer, for having redeemed them."[2] Even now, in our current prayer book, "Confession is the obverse of thanksgiving; to give thanks for redemption is to acknowledge one's sinfulness."[3] The confession is usually omitted from the liturgy for feasts of the church year, particularly during Eastertide. When the church is singing its most joyous songs of praise, the confession is judged to be out of place, perhaps even inappropriate. "Alleluia, Christ is risen," the priest sings; "The Lord is risen indeed, alleluia" the people respond. We omit the confession and focus solely on the joyful part of the resurrection story.

But perhaps this is a mistake. The joy that Christians feel in their contemplation of the empty tomb is complicated by the fact that the risen Jesus is confrontational: on that first Easter, and even now, he confronts us about our wrongdoing. Former Archbishop of Canterbury, Rowan Williams, reflects on this in his book *Resurrection*.[4] He notes that most of the post-resurrection encounters with Jesus in all four gospel accounts and in the Acts of the Apostles were between the risen Jesus and people who participated in his betrayal, trial, and death. The Risen One appears to repentant betrayers—the disciples who ran away when he was arrested, or flatly denied their association with him. He then appears (through his spirit-filled Jerusalem followers) to the unrepentant authorities who had handed Jesus over to judgment and crucifixion and remained opposed to the Jesus Movement. And he finally appears to the apostle Paul, who never met Jesus before the resurrection but was confronted by a vision of the risen Christ on the road to Damascus. Jesus is merciful and breathes peace to his followers, but he is nevertheless profoundly unnerving. His ability to appear among them, effortlessly moving through locked doors, frightens them. Williams's risen Jesus is troubling, an enigmatic figure confronting these people—and through them, us—with complicity in his death. Because of this, according to Williams, the community of the Risen One is always a community of forgiven people. Our harrowing recollection of our own wrongdoing is never far from our prayerful consciousness.

Williams's key insight is that, with the notable exception of the faithful women (and especially Mary Magdalene), the resurrection is announced first to the offenders, the wrongdoers, the guilty ones. Nowhere is this revealed more vividly than in John 21:15–19:

> When they had finished breakfast, Jesus said to Simon Peter, "Simon son of John, do you love me more than these?" He said to him, "Yes, Lord; you know that I love you." Jesus said to him, "Feed my lambs." A second time he said to him, "Simon son of John, do you love me?" He said to him, "Yes, Lord; you know that I love you." Jesus said to him, "Tend my sheep." He said to him the third time, "Simon son of John, do you love me?" Peter felt hurt because he said to him the third time, "Do you love me?" And he said to him, "Lord, you know everything; you know that I love you." Jesus said to him, "Feed my sheep. Very truly, I tell you, when you were younger, you used to fasten your own belt and to go wherever you wished. But when you grow old, you will stretch out your hands, and someone else will fasten a belt around you and take you where you do not wish to go." (He said this to indicate the kind of death by which he would glorify God.) After this he said to him, "Follow me."

This passage merits close reading. First, note how Jesus addresses Peter not by the name "Peter," or "Rock," but by his given name, Simon, son of John. Why remove the title that Jesus himself gave to him? This is sometimes interpreted to mean that Jesus was simply meeting Peter where Peter was in that moment. Filled with remorse, doubting and even despairing about the way everything seemed to have ended, Peter had gone back to being merely "Simon." ("I am going fishing," he says, earlier in the chapter, sounding a note of discouraged resignation.) But in my reading, Jesus is being both confrontational and personal. When you want to discuss something significant with someone, you sometimes change how you address them. My father would occasionally call me "Stephen Daniel," and that never failed to get my attention.

Second, notice that Jesus prescribes a repair behavior each time he confronts Peter with his wrongdoing. Each time Jesus asks "Do you love me?" (one time for each of Peter's denials), and Peter replies in the affirmative, Jesus then tells Peter to do something: "Feed my lambs," "Tend my sheep," "Feed my sheep." Jesus tells Peter to serve and lead the community Jesus is leaving behind. Peter's amends for his denials are made with the whole body of Christ, not just Jesus himself. And he is sent on this mission of amends by Jesus, the person he harmed.

So Peter has begun the work of remorse. He felt hurt as Jesus took up the painful topic of his betrayal ("feeling sorry"). He followed Jesus through a step-by-step description of what needed to happen to repair his betrayals ("thinking sorry"). He expressed authentic love to Jesus (in my reading, this counts as a form of apology, of "saying sorry"). And he was given a mission ("doing sorry").

But even as we trace Peter's experience of remorse, we remember: this is an Easter story! It is proclaimed in the middle of the most festive weeks of our liturgical year. Peter's story culminates in gladness. He is the chief apostle, filled with the spirit, sent by the risen Christ to proclaim the Good News. His joy is made complete.

This is not just the story of one person, though. In his appearance to Peter, Jesus directs the ethic of remorse to the whole community. The love that Peter expresses here—his way of "saying sorry," and the work of amends that inevitably follows—is to be shown not just to Jesus himself, but to everyone Jesus claims as his own. The power of this repair redounds far beyond this little clutch of fishermen at breakfast by the sea. That it touches others is right and good, because Peter harmed the whole community around Jesus when he denied his Lord three times. And so, when Peter takes up the mantle of leadership as an apostle, his whole identity as a leader grows and flourishes as the fruit of his remorse, and for the benefit and deep gladness of the whole community.

The joy of Easter, then, is always embedded with the trauma of the human behaviors that necessitated Easter in the first place. The joy always follows sorrow. Or better said, the sorrow deepens the joy. Christ emerges from the tomb with wounded hands. He cooks breakfast for a pensive group of fishermen who had just decided to go back to their nets, disappointed, disoriented, and exhausted by all that had happened. And so I wonder: why do some Christian communities focus only on the joyful themes of the Easter season? In the seven weeks of Easter, churches sing festive songs, hang and wear bright colors, and say glad prayers of thanksgiving, and so they should! Easter is preceded by Lent, a season that encourages introspection and confession, intended to prepare the assembly for the glad Easter feast. "Christ is risen!" we proclaim, punctuating the news with a happy exclamation mark. Yes. *And yet*, the joy of the first Easter came when the risen Christ confronted the followers who had betrayed him, and led them through the work of remorse. We may find that pausing for confession—even and perhaps especially during the Easter season—may best prepare us to recognize the presence of the Risen One in our midst, and also form us as God's remorseful yet joyful people.

One of my Easter Day experiences carried this particular Easter joy, the joy that is deepened by sorrow. In my first year in seminary, I served as a bread minister on Easter Day at Washington National Cathedral. Many hundreds of people formed lines to receive bread and drink from the cup. Communion stations dotted the room. As each person came forward and extended a hand to receive the bread, their facial expressions were striking: rarely did someone offer an uncomplicated smile. There seemed to be an almost haunted look in the eyes of many people. They kept coming, rows and rows of people, and almost to a person they made eye contact, and in that encounter they seemed to be looking longingly for something. Perhaps they wanted an answer or two. Perhaps they could scarcely believe or trust what had just been preached to them. Certainly, many were confused about practical matters in such a huge room bustling with activity. But their silent progression through the room may have proclaimed a deeper truth about the meaning of Easter Day. It is not just a glib party for a redeemed people no longer troubled by human wrongdoing. Nor is it a funeral! It is something between those two poles. Or it transcends them entirely. Williams touches a truth in his portrayal of the Risen One as confrontational, strange, arresting: can these congregants truly encounter the One who knows their stories, and saves them from their sins? Confession and forgiveness during Eastertide may help facilitate this very encounter. Confession and forgiveness may even be more of an Easter rite than a Lenten one!

WEEPING IN THE NIGHT, JOY IN THE MORNING

Healthy remorse offers both sorrow and joy. Both experiences are common in a healthy, honest spiritual life in which a person (or group or large community) wants to grow, to be transformed, to be and feel better. We can trace this pattern of sorrow and joy in Psalm 30, a psalm of thanksgiving that fully acknowledges how dreadful life can sometimes be, and how God leads us from the sorrow of sin into the joy of forgiveness, reconciliation, and restoration.

> 2   O Lord my God, I cried to you for help,
>   and you have healed me.
> 3   O Lord, you brought up my soul from Sheol,
>   restored me to life from among those gone down to
>   the Pit.
>
> 4   Sing praises to the Lord, O you his faithful ones,
>   and give thanks to his holy name.
> 5   For his anger is but for a moment;
>   his favor is for a lifetime.
>   Weeping may linger for the night,
>   but joy comes with the morning . . .
>
> 11   You have turned my mourning into dancing;
>   you have taken off my sackcloth
>   and clothed me with joy,
> 12   so that my soul may praise you and not be silent.
>   O Lord my God, I will give thanks to you forever.

God's anger lasts "but a moment," and God's favor "is for a lifetime." Though it's hard to know for sure the reason for the original psalmist's suffering, the subtitle on the psalm is "A song at the dedication of the Temple. Of David." One can imagine that even if the writer of the psalm was not King David, this psalm is inspired by David's experience of remorse and restoration. Interestingly, about midway through the psalm we hear about the psalmist's former happiness: "As for me," the psalmist sings, "I said in my prosperity, 'I shall not be moved.'" But then in the very next verse, God hides God's face, and the psalmist is "dismayed." (In the Episcopal *Book of Common Prayer*, "dismayed" is translated as "filled with fear.") Something happens to the psalmist that causes God to withdraw, or perhaps the psalmist does something to break relationship with God. But to their immense relief, God is faithful, and God restores them to health. And God does this in response to the psalmist crying out (could the psalmist have been "saying sorry"?). At that point the psalmist is overwhelmed with joy: "You have turned my mourning into dancing; you have taken off my sackcloth and clothed me with joy."

This joy is powerful. It is much stronger even than the "punch of shame" I suffered as I awakened from my DUI nightmare-come-true. Imagine a "punch" of joy that doesn't immediately dissipate, that only deepens over time. When we feel, think, say, and do sorry, we find that the AA Promises, written with confidence and deep gladness, are almost an understatement. Think of Peter and the others on the day of Pentecost. They are exultant, caught up in a fever of joy that runs deep. Peter and the others (with the notable exception of the women in their company) had betrayed Jesus, and not long before this gathering had been cowering in fear behind locked doors. But the risen Christ has confronted them, and they have done the work of remorse. They are filled with God's spirit. And so this great gladness of God overwhelms them, and they eagerly hurry outside to share the good news with the world.

This is the blessing of healthy remorse. This is the gift of honest apology. This is intense grace, lavishly offered to human beings. I have been preoccupied with remorse for nearly a decade now, for only one reason: so that my soul—and the souls of many others—will praise God and not be silent, and give thanks to the Lord our God forever, our joy made complete.

NOTES

PREFACE

1   Alcoholics Anonymous World Services, *Alcoholics Anonymous, 4th ed.* (New York: Alcoholics Anonymous World Services, 2001), 562.

2   The Episcopal Church, *Enriching Our Worship 1* (New York: Church Publishing, 1998), 19.

CHAPTER 1

1   St. Anselm, *Meditations and Prayers to the Holy Trinity and Our Lord Jesus Christ* (London: James Parker & Co., 1872), 33.

2   Robert Francis Capon, *The Mystery of Christ, and Why We Don't Get It* (Grand Rapids, MI: Wm. B. Eerdmans Publishing, 1993), 9.

3   Capon, *The Mystery of Christ*, 27.

4   Fleming Rutledge, *The Crucifixion: Understanding the Death of Jesus Christ* (Grand Rapids, MI: Wm. B. Eerdmans Publishing, 2015), 170.

CHAPTER 2

1   John Perry, *The Problem of the Essential Indexical, and Other Essays* (New York: Oxford University Press, 1993), 33.

2   "Ah, Holy Jesus, How Hast Thou Offended," in *The Hymnal 1982* (New York: Church Hymnal Corporation, 1982, hymn 158).

3   *The West Wing*, season 3, episode 11, "H-Con 172," directed by Vincent Miciano, aired January 9, 2002, on NBC.

4   The Episcopal Church, *The Book of Common Prayer* (New York: Church Hymnal Corporation, 1979), 448.

5   Johann Heermann, trans. Robert Bridges, text in the public domain, in *The Hymnal 1982*, hymn 158.

CHAPTER 3

1   Lindy West, *Shrill: Notes from a Loud Woman* (New York: Hachette Books, 2016).

2   West, *Shrill*, 244.

3   Lindy West, "If You Don't Have Anything Nice to Say, SAY IT IN ALL CAPS. Act One: Ask Not for Whom the Bell Trolls; It Trolls for Thee," episode 545, *This American Life*, January 23, 2015, accessed May 18, 2022,

https://www.thisamericanlife.org/545/if-you-dont-have-anything-nice-to-say-say-it-in-all-caps/act-one-0.

4   West, *Shrill*, 252.

5   West, 254.

6   Stephen Harper, *"Prime Minister Offers Full Apology on Be-half of Canadians for the Indian Residential Schools System,"* Government of Canada website, June 11, 2008, accessed August 8, 2022, https://www.rcaanc-cirnac.gc.ca/eng/110 0100015644/1571589171655.

CHAPTER 4

1   John M. Gottman and Julie Schwartz Gottman, *Gottman Method Couples Therapy: Level 3 Clinical Training Manual*, section 13. Seattle: The Gottman Institute, Inc., 2014).

2   Sue Johnson, *Hold Me Tight: Seven Conversations for a Life-time of Love* (New York: Little, Brown, 2008).

3   Jacques Kelly, "Thomas Palermo, Software Engineer and Cyclist," *Baltimore Sun*, December 30, 2014.

4   The Archives of the Episcopal Church, "The Acts of Con-vention," July 2015, accessed November 11, 2019, https://episcopalarchives.org/cgi-bin/acts/acts_search.pl.

5   The word "accident" is troublesome when used to describe a drunk-driving event. If a sober driver misjudges the angle of a left turn and strikes a barrier, that can uncontroversially be called an accident. But to drink and drive, or text and drive, and by doing so kill another human being: is this, solely, an accident?

6   The Episcopal Church, *The Book of Common Prayer* (New York: Church Publishing, 1979), 214.

CHAPTER 5

1   Alcoholics Anonymous World Services, *Alcoholics Anonymous*, 4th ed. (New York: Alcoholics Anonymous World Services, 2001), 83–84.
2   Marion J. Hatchett, *Commentary on the American Prayer Book* (New York: HarperCollins Publishers, 1995), 341.
3   Hatchett, *Commentary,* 342.
4   Rowan Williams, *Resurrection: Interpreting the Easter Gospel* (London: Darton, Longman & Todd, 1982).

RECOMMENDED RESOURCES

THEOLOGY OF REMORSE

Anselm of Canterbury. *Meditations and Prayers to the Holy Trinity and Our Lord Jesus Christ.* London: James Parker and Co., 1872.

St. Anselm can sometimes be a gloomy companion, but his prayers are nonetheless useful for private devotion. He certainly explores his own feelings with courage and honesty, and he does not shrink from the moral need to hold himself accountable. He writes with deep faith and keen insight.

Capon, Robert Francis. *The Mystery of Christ, and Why We Don't Get It.* Grand Rapids, MI: Wm. B. Eerdmans Publishing, 1993.

Robert Capon is a more cheerful friend if you are exploring the topic of remorse. He rejects shame for the harmful (and often self-centered!) waste of time that it is, and he offers a bracing and refreshing take on the Bible, worship, and Christian life in general. If he were the priest hearing my confession, I would not fear his judgment, and would respect his advice, even as I took issue with one or two of his points.

Newbigin, Lesslie. *The Gospel in a Pluralist Society.* Grand Rapids, MI: Wm. B. Eerdmans Publishing, 1989.

Lesslie Newbigin's insights on the cross embrace remorse as an appropriate response to the crucifixion. For Newbigin, the cross is where God's grace intersects most powerfully with human sin, and if that makes you squeamish because of your concerns about the theology of atonement, keep reading. Newbigin's theology affirms the dignity of human nature, and offers a hopeful and positive view of redemption.

Prejean, Helen. *Dead Man Walking: The Eyewitness Account of the Death Penalty that Sparked a National Debate.* New York: Vintage Books, 1993.

Robbins, Tim. *Dead Man Walking.* Los Angeles: PolyGram Filmed Entertainment, 1995.

Helen Prejean, both in her books and in the film produced by Tim Robbins, leads wrongdoers along the path of healthy remorse, pushing far beyond her assigned task, which was simply to offer pastoral care to death-row inmates. She wants to confront them and get them to admit their guilt, for the benefit not only of their victims' families, but for their own salvation as well. Prejean, a prophet of our time, has gone on to advocate for death-row inmates both guilty and innocent. She is a leading figure in the work to abolish the death penalty.

Rutledge, Fleming. *The Crucifixion: Understanding the Death of Jesus Christ*. Grand Rapids, MI: Wm. B. Eerdmans Publishing, 2015.

Fleming Rutledge writes at length and with skill on the crucifixion, often embracing rather conservative views. For example, she considers the substitutionary theory of atonement, and offers a strong defense of it. Along the way, she explores human wrongdoing in a way that truly acknowledges the damage it has caused, and challenges her reader to take seriously the moral and ethical implications of the death of Jesus Christ.

West, Lindy. *Shrill: Notes from a Loud Woman*. New York: Hachette Books, 2016.

Lindy West offers strange but refreshing company on this list. Her memoir is not about remorse, and she is not Christian, but her story about the internet troll is remarkable. I don't think I have read a more compelling story about the power of *saying sorry*.

Williams, Rowan. *Resurrection: Interpreting the Easter Gospel.* London: Darton, Longman & Todd, 1982.

Rowan Williams explores the resurrection with a pastor's heart, and portrays the risen Christ as an unsettling, even upsetting stranger who confronts us with peace, but also challenge. In Williams's hands, Easter is not just a jubilant celebration—it is something *better* than that.

REMORSE, GENDER, AND RACE

Cone, James. "Theology's Greatest Sin: Silence in the Face of White Supremacy." *Black Theology* 2, no. 2 (2004): 139–52.

James Cone critiques white theologians, focusing on their silent tolerance of—and subsequent complicity in—the evil of white supremacy. White theologians tend to avoid the topic completely, likely because they enjoy white privilege and therefore don't have to talk about it, it arouses feelings of guilt, they are afraid of black rage, and they are "not prepared for a radical redistribution of wealth and power" (p. 139). Cone's perspective informs our work on remorse by focusing on systems of power that privilege some and not others. Remorse is never simply the work an offender does to repair the damage he caused: power and privilege always complicate the picture.

Johnson, Elizabeth. *She Who Is: The Mystery of God in Feminist Theological Discourse.* New York: The Crossroad Publishing Co., 2007.

Meeks, Catherine. *An Exploration of Reparations at Virginia Theological Seminary: A Webinar.* Alexandria: Virginia Theological Seminary, 2020. Accessed April 4, 2020, https://www.facebook.com/VirginiaTheologicalSeminary/videos/2483162421997692/.

Catherine Meeks participates in a webinar that considers the reparations project at Virginia Theological Seminary. This reparations project is an example of an educational institution doing the work of remorse—specifically *doing sorry*. In a way James Cone would likely appreciate, it is a complicated project.

Ramshaw, Gail. *Under the Tree of Life: The Religion of a Feminist Christian.* Akron, OH: OSL Publications, 2003.

"Wrongdoing" is a complicated term. Feminist theologians rightly critique androcentric theologies of remorse that focus exclusively on bad behavior and the need to apologize. Elizabeth Johnson and Gail Ramshaw offer feminist interpretations of sin and grace, noting that the chief sin of women may be passivity: the sin of submissively diminishing the self. Should women really learn how to be better at apologizing? Women may already be apologizing too much.

REMORSE IN THE COMMUNION OF SAINTS

This book focuses on remorse in human life, but not in the life to come. These authors explore the idea of remorse among the whole communion of saints.

Battle, Michael. *Heaven and Earth: God's Call to Community in the Book of Revelation.* Louisville, KY: Westminster John Knox Press, 2017.

Michael Battle examines the practice of *ubuntu*, which joins a community in mutually respectful dialogue, honoring and deepening their identity as one people. But Battle's understanding of *ubuntu* expands to include heaven: transcending the simplistic vision of heaven as an uncomplicated paradise, God and human beings continue to "toil together in the salvation of creation" (p. 140).

Lewis, C. S. *The Great Divorce: A Dream.* New York: HarperCollins Publishers, 2001.

C. S. Lewis, writing in the popular vein, imagines a bus that transports residents of hell to the edge of heaven. They are met by heavenly souls who greet them and invite them to stay. Lewis imagines various encounters, and various responses by heaven's visitors. Some reject the invitation and get back on the bus. Others are uncertain, and we don't learn their ultimate fate. Still others accept the invitation and are transformed into saints. Lewis is particularly skillful in his exploration of honest remorse in these stories. Often a soul need only admit their own mistake, and the blessings of heaven are theirs.

Thiel, John. *Icons of Hope: The "Last Things" in Catholic Imagination.* Notre Dame, IN: University of Notre Dame Press, 2013.

John Thiel notices that in the Apostles' Creed, the line "the forgiveness of sins" is said between "the communion of saints" and "the resurrection of the body." He interprets this not merely as a list of things the faithful believe, but an intentional juxtaposition of heavenly life with forgiveness. In Thiel's vision, souls after death continue to ask each other for forgiveness. In my way of saying it, we continue to feel, think, say, and do sorry even after death. However that may sound, this is not sad: again, remorse leads to deep joy, and a vision of heaven as a place where people seek forgiveness is if anything happier than one of heaven as a city of eternal bliss. One could even imagine that, in Thiel's vision, injuries that were deemed beyond repair on earth can be addressed: a murderer can approach her victim with honest remorse.

Von Balthasar, Hans Urs. *Mysterium Paschale.* Translated by Aiden Nichols. San Francisco: Ignatius Press, 2005.

Hans Urs von Balthasar reflects on Holy Saturday, a day on the church calendar but also a day that can be understood as eternal. On Holy Saturday, Jesus of Nazareth lies dead in the tomb, but Jesus Christ is harrowing hell, confronting all who have broken their relationship with God, inviting them to repent. Taken together, the visions of Battle, Lewis, Thiel, and von Balthasar imagine remorse comprehensively, existing in heaven, earth, and hell.

RESOURCES FROM THE FIELD OF PSYCHOTHERAPY

Abrahms Spring, Janis. *How Can I Forgive You: The Courage to Forgive, the Freedom Not To.* New York: HarperCollins Publishers, 2004.

Janis Abrams Spring considers forgiveness from her perspective as a couples therapist who specializes in major betrayals. Rejecting the idea of unconditional forgiveness, Abrams offers two healthy options for responding to a betrayal: acceptance and genuine forgiveness. In acceptance, the hurt person does not forgive the offender, or even ask anything at all of them, but works on their own to make sense of what happened and move on in a healthy way. Genuine forgiveness is similar to acceptance, except that the offender is highly involved, helping the hurt person follow the steps of acceptance and eventually earning their forgiveness.

Gottman, John, and Nan Silver. *What Makes Love Last? How to Build Trust and Avoid Betrayal.* New York: Simon & Schuster, 2012.

John Gottman and his wife Julie Gottman are leading figures in the field of couples therapy, offering a comprehensive method of treatment for couples grounded in John's extensive research and Julie's clinical expertise. Their method focuses on the couple's friendship as the core of a healthy relationship, and in *What Makes Love Last?* John writes in the popular vein about how a couple can "turn toward each other," often by doing the work of honest apology.

Johnson, Sue. *Hold Me Tight: Seven Conversations for a Lifetime of Love.* New York: Little, Brown, 2008.

Sue Johnson, a Canadian couples therapist, is a leading writer and clinician who created "Emotionally

Focused Therapy," which helps couples get in touch with their attachment needs. She skillfully helps couples access the deeper emotions behind a conflict and, by sharing these feelings, the couple draws closer together and begins to heal. She wrote *Hold Me Tight* in the popular vein, and it offers insights for all relationships, not just married couples.

RESOURCES ON ALCOHOLISM, RECOVERY, AND FAITH

Alcoholics Anonymous World Services. *Living Sober.* New York: Alcoholics Anonymous World Services, 1975, 2012.

   Living Sober is a small book that advises recovering alcoholics about many practical matters, particularly in early recovery. It's a good resource for those who are "white-knuckling" their recovery—struggling to stay sober, and in need of basic advice. It can inform non-alcoholics as well, giving them a good perspective on the challenges of sobriety.

Knudsen, Chilton R., and Nancy Van Dyke Platt. *So You Think You Don't Know One? Addiction and Recovery in Clergy and Congregations.* New York: Morehouse Publishing, 2010.

Nancy Van Dyke Platt and Chilton Knudsen address the many problems caused by untreated or unacknowledged addiction in clergy and the congregations they serve. Addiction can often be the "elephant in the room" for congregations who are afraid to discuss frightening topics openly, particularly when the person with the problem is their clergy.

Rohr, Richard. *Breathing under Water: Spirituality and the Twelve Steps.* Cincinnati: St. Anthony Messenger Press, 2011.

Richard Rohr reflects deeply on the AA Twelve Steps and how they can guide a healthy spiritual practice of sobriety and recovery. He generalizes the concepts of the Twelve Steps beyond just substance abuse, connecting the concept of "addiction" to the universal human problem of sin. Rohr does this with his typical warmth and wisdom, tackling challenging topics with a pastor's heart.